RELIQUIAE

Landscape   Nature   Mythology

CORBEL STONE PRESS

Reliquiae

Volume 9 Number 1

ISSN 2398–7359

Edited by Autumn Richardson & Richard Skelton
Published by Corbel Stone Press

ISBN 978-1-9160951-6-8

1

Sarah Westcott
Bud

2

Kim Dorman
Kerala Journal (Excerpts)

6

Rabindranath Tagore
Stray Birds (Excerpts)

11

Paul Prudence
Figured Stones (Excerpts)

20

From Kwakiutl Folklore
Klawulacha / Song of the Totem-Pole

*

25
Rebekah Clayton
yew

26
Gaspar Orozco
*El Libro de los Espejismos /
The Book of Mirages (Excerpts)
(Translated by Ilana Luna)*

40
From Navajo Folklore
Dsichl Biyin / Mountain-Song

44
Don Domanski
Two Poems

*

49
William Tyler Olcott
The Pleiades

64
Jennifer Spector
Hithe (Excerpts)

*

71

Frances Horovitz
Four Poems

78

Rebecca Drake
Awntyrs, women (Excerpt)

80

Isidro Li
Four Poems

84

From The Tanner Bede
Caedmon's Hymn
(Translated by Peter O'Leary)

86

Frater Acher
The Straight Line is a Trap

*

95

Triin Paja

Four Poems

102

From Navajo Folklore

Dsichl Biyin / Mountain-Song

114

Shash Trevett

Waratah

*

119
Don Domanski
Pleiades

122
Penelope Shuttle
the half-guest

123
Robin Walter
Six Poems

130
Donald A. Mackenzie
*Babylonian and Egyptian
Astronomy (Excerpt)*

*

143
Sarah Berti
Five Poems

150
From Navajo Folklore
Naye-e Sin / War-Song

154
Constance Naden
Four Poems

160
Gaspar Orozco
Alminar / Minaret (Excerpt)
(Translated by Ilana Luna)

162
Elizabeth-Jane Burnett
Two Poems

*

167
Michael Goodfellow
Book of Days

170
Erin Wilson
Three Poems

174
Kabir
Five Poems

180
Arvind Krishna Mehrotra
Lockdown Garden (Excerpt)

184
Richard Skinner
Two Poems

186
Alton Melvar M. Dapanas
Self-Portrait as Wak-wak

*

191
Gustav Meyrink
Fakir Paths
(Introduced and translated by
Frater Acher)

*

215
End Matter
Notes & Bibliography

*Each section is completed
by a selection of Hopi words*

Reliquiae interleaves eco-
logically aware writing from
the past and present, rang-
ing from the ethnological
to the philosophical, the
lyrical to the visionary. It
is published biannually,
in May and November.

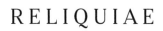

RELIQUIAE

Sarah Westcott
Bud

There are parts of our bodies we will never know.

The soul, animate,

needs a body to rove in the animal way
as buds split with the violence of dawn.

What do we do to each other? That we cannot do to ourselves

in the soft-locked rooms of our bodies,
         such ministrations —
                           dear bodies we grub for you
in the dark soil, the dark beds, where children wait for
                                        mothers —

*

I hold a robin, eyes filling with cloud,
ribbed soft breast —

What last song did it put in the air?

   Our last words are coming,

buds splitting their song   sweet mercy of our bodies
                                       falling open.

Kim Dorman
Kerala Journal (Excerpts)

Venus appears over
the cowshed

like an ancient sign.

*

Slow dusk. Egrets arise
from paddy fields.

The sky is clear. I no longer
think of America.

Sitting on veranda steps,
I look up at the stars.

    *

the
root

of
the

word
is

the
breath

*

morning sky
the spare calligraphy
of crows

Rabindranath Tagore
Stray Birds (Excerpts)

14

The mystery of creation is like
the darkness of night—it is great.
Delusions of knowledge are like
the fog of the morning.

47

Shadow, with her veil drawn,
follows Light in secret meekness,
with her silent steps of love.

64

Thank the flame for its light,
but do not forget the lampholder
standing in the shade with
constancy of patience.

70

Where is the fountain that throws
up these flowers in a ceaseless
outbreak of ecstasy?

72

In my solitude of heart I feel the
sigh of this widowed evening veiled
with mist and rain.

81

What is this unseen flame of
darkness whose sparks are the
stars?

82

Let life be beautiful like summer
flowers and death like autumn
leaves.

104

The music of the far-away summer
flutters around the autumn seeking
its former nest.

119

The night kisses the fading day
whispering to his ear, 'I am death,
your mother. I am to give you fresh
birth.'

142

Let me think that there is one
among those stars that guides my
life through the dark unknown.

Paul Prudence
Figured Stones (Excerpts)

Bloodstones (The Walled City of Changhua)

With blood-red flecks and arterial systems, Changhua Stones,
also known as bloodstones, offer to the eye a potent pathol-
ogy of lithos. In these stones it seems that the very body of
the earth has been cut open to reveal a tree of bloody dia-
tremes; a spread of vivid streaks pouring through the earth's
cadaver. Through rock capillaries, these threads of red form
a freckled sluice that leaks through the bruised peach blurs
of cytoplasmic urges and into the thirsts of metamorphic
veins. If the ragged clefts in Taihu stones suggest the forms
of ancient bones, and the fissured curves of Anhui rocks the
shapes of ravaged skulls, then Changhua Stones propose the
frozen flow of earth-borne ichor.

Red in rock has forever symbolised the idea of blood, and
blood in rock enlivens the idea of the earth as a living, dead,
or mythic body. In ancient Rome red-flecked stones were

worn as amulets to stem the loss of blood. In India they were used to staunch a bleeding wound when impressed upon the skin.[1] The Incas believed that the blood of their gods flowed through precious stones,[2] and for medieval Christians the stains of red in stone symbolised drops of blood from their saviour's crucifixion.

Bloodstone, another name for heliotrope, gets its speckled red from smears of haematite embedded in the stone. This oxide shares its etymology with haemoglobin, the molecule that transports iron through the living veins of every animal. And so it seems that geology is predisposed to reciprocate the strategies of biology. In the forking veins of planar fractures, and with a texture of an ancient flow long ceased, lithic blood courses through the earth's hepatic portals to create its own anatomical designs. Thermal forces distil the lithic plasma through thin-veined walls to reservoirs of crack-sealed space where that *colluvia* of plasma pools. A seepage that, in turn, turns stars within the earth's unconscious sediments.[3]

In ancient China, bloodstone was carved into sacred seals which, when impressed upon strips of bamboo, created glistening characters with a waxy sheen. This 'blood writing' can be traced back more than three thousand years to when it was used to write prognostications on oracles of bone. On scapulas and on the shells of turtles a magic writing came to life and signed the way to more complex scripts which were then transferred to stones.

The designs of hand-carved bloodstone can be *so* arresting that even the most questing eye sacrifices all other interests and forgoes all other stimuli to peruse the details. Lavish curves and sculpted waves suggest the forms of chambered hearts and ornamental lairs with streams of fractal smoke. Carved lines trace spiral-bound paths and swirled inflections hinting at some mad internal logic—the carver's hand invoked by unseen forces which emanate from within the rock. An artistry guided by the divinity of blood to accentuate geology's inner solicitations. Bloodstone was commonly carved into elaborate scenes and ornate landscapes: tiny villages hanging from precipices amid vast promontories. Animals would often haunt these scenes, especially birds and dragons. According to a legend it was a golden pheasant that spilt its blood upon a mountain after being bitten by a snake — its blood flowing into the veins of rock to infuse it with that trademark bloody flair.[4]

Red lights in southern skies. Dream cell necropoli of flame-forged visions awaken memories of flushed horizons. Inside a bloodstone, smoke is billowing across the sky. Specular lines of half-forgotten paths thread their way through rock to a sleeping city where sun-baked walls feed clinging vines that twine their stems through Lycian tombs. The walled city of Changhua is a blurred mirage hanging in a bloodshot sky. The sun, a half-closed eye, recedes behind the city's walls — suspended like a melting jewel over russet brickwork. And as it moves to safety in falling light it leaves behind an emblem of its herald: an ancient shiny beetle that rolls another different, smaller sun along its path. The city, now a blackened crystal, folds its shadows inwards. Moonlight spills through the cracks in mortar projecting maps upon the quartz-encrusted rubble. Eyes glitter with a green spark in the streets below, before the city retires to sleep. Flares criss-cross and cross-hatch the city's archive as ley lines light up for returning spirits. Cerise and copper holding patterns hang their emblems skywards — runways cleared for long-haul spectres returning from their wild-fire dreams.

The narratives of bloodstone unfold in numerous permutations. Blurred outlines diffuse to scenes of minarets and silhouettes of colonnades. Dreaming lines draw the skyward-pointing arrows of sun-stoked pylons. Plan upon plan, dream upon dream, layered images reveal the compound lines of mounds and tombs and mausoleums—a *fata morgana* of ancient towns made into a single reddened city and arranged according to the rules of geomancy. Here and there shadows race across the squares and plazas—shadows hatched as ghosted zones on breathing maps. Figures breathe out their wreaths of rock-cut spells in damask smoke. A rubescent trail to catch a current and to connect all dreams. A sign to mark a place of dreaming; a beacon for the dreaming space. A script to score the ember fever; a shift from rock to living fire.

The crimson finch flies east, the red-veined darter, west. The calisto newt and scarlet ibis ignore the movements of the magnet. All reds lead to the stellar mansions of ghosts and corpses, to where the night has become a captive to the tender tint of dawn, and to where dreams dissolve to scattered rust. Red mites have traced their final lines and formed their final runes. The cardinal has inscribed, in flight, the terminating circle. Today, nothing much remains of the famous scenes of fired-up glory; mining has destroyed the ruby palaces and collapsed the city's towers. The ground is sunken, the city's walls are ruined and the mother-lodes are empty. All that is left of the temples are their outlines marked in stone. Nature's teeming generosity has been reduced and levelled to a plain of ruins; only faint inscriptions recall the former glory of the famous walled city of Changhua.

Time Compiled

In contemplating rocks we must shift the tiny gears of our watches to cycles of such magnitude that the seconds now seem to move so slowly as to appear to not move at all. Geological time, a paradox of both stasis and immense unending movement, encapsulates *all* time and for this reason it has the *assured anonymity of oblivion*. Rocks tell us that time is a thing intangible but yet fatal, something invisible but yet vivid with such a devastating effect. Yet, in the presence of the two, it's the authority of time that becomes uncertain for only against the grave durations of geology can time's true mettle be judged. Geology makes time take stock of itself—it is the only thing that can give time any sense of certainty. Take away the aeons and the eras, the Archaeans and the Hadeans, remove the periods and epochs, the Cambrians and the Silurians, and you will see that there really is *no* time. Geology is so obdurate in this respect that the only way *it* can exist is by the clever trick of flowing through itself (while remaining fixed like water). Geology suspends time but it also moulds it, and it pushes time to near breaking point. The play with time in rock has been traditionally appreciated, so much so that all around the world there are collectors of certain stones who assure themselves of great longevity just by being in proximity to beloved pieces. Here is a world of rooms with rocks and people suspended in their vortices of a *time-just-stopped*.

Rocks condense time by converging their immensities with our small cycles. They compile the aeons and—bearing witness to the vast dimensions of the stellar constellations—they condense the orogenic complexities into a single glance. Timescales mingle and mate in the mind when the textural promiscuity of rocks are beamed to the eye and the aeons and epochs are bound into a single thread. The Palaeolithic crumples, the Mesolithic cracks and the Neolithic zooms towards us. By reaching deep into our imaginations a rock momentarily relinquishes its place in oblivion and, enmeshed within the spectres of our fascinations, it connects to *our* time. Momentarily it remains captive to *our* sense of space before pressing onwards into the empty distance. Rocks may peer across eternities but in their solemn stillness they bring to us an essence of a moment when the eye of time casts its clearest and most untainted vision—an impression cast upon the mizzen shroud of perpetuity where the vaguest hints of some future port of call are given. Here are the glimmers of an Archaean proposition firing forwards to its future destination—to celestial navigation and radiometric dating.

With the discovery of *deep-time* the Scottish geologist James Hutton unbracketed geology from its sure sense of belonging and absolved it from any sense of origin.[5] When he stared in awe at Siccar Point his eyes drew a blank and his mind reeled backwards to a time both unfathomable and unknowable—a time ripped up from its rails. In Hutton's own immortal words, geology had 'no vestige of a beginning, no prospect of an end'. Until this point, time had been bound by theological dimensions, fixed in place by the doctrines of religion.[6] It was Hutton's friend, John Playfair, who remarked upon this new-found heresy that 'the mind seemed to grow giddy by looking so far into the abyss...' No wonder that theology was so appalled with deep-time, carrying as it did the connotations of a prior world of dark and empty spirits. The path to Eden now seemed to trace back to an abyss devoid of any temporal referent, a place of devils and hell-bound demons.

In their perfect garden-labyrinths made of stone, the artisans of the Ming-Qing era rebuilt the cosmos on an earthly scale and conceived of it as timeless. By multiplying space with a maze-like repetition, their gardens confounded any sense of standard temporal flow. The word *labyrinth* can be translated into Chinese as *migong*, which means 'a perplexing palace'.[7] And these perplexing palaces were aimed at elevating one's experience beyond the earthly world to

a time suspended, a time held forever in an instant—the
Blakeian time deferred. This absolute non-reducible time
can be separated from the mythic concept of eternity as the
Heideggerian 'original' time which leads to the '"ecstases"
of temporality'.[8]

Figured stones connect human time with that primordial
time.[9] They infer both Heraclitus's axiom of mutability (the
coursing flux of flowing time) and Parmenides's eternal stasis
of our being (the 'all time' of the single glance). Figured
stones mock our quests of becoming by evoking the *ecstasis*
of being. And in the ecstasy of time where our becoming *is*
our being, we become like rock, static within the instant,
equipoised and immune to entropy, a cosmic dot without a
measurement of movement.

But, perhaps a rock is not so much an emblem of these
hard-to-grasp eternities but an emblem of eternity's own
forgetfulness—or its slow realisation of what it really is. A
rock, as a fragment of Earth's own memory, only recollects
itself in the presence of *a* consciousness that can perceive it,
because nothing else exists in time's forgetfulness, not even
the stars who must await *our* invented fates. Time *is* stern
but it takes a mortal to transmogrify its work into a thing
with living spirit. Only a soul that dies can transform a thing
that lasts forever with a spell or with a vision into something
conscious. And so as *memento mori* (or the inverted signs
of death) rocks may symbolise our mortal struggles but they
also breathe life into our immortal souls. In the company of
rocks we create parity between our transience and that essen-
tial emptiness of unceasing durations.

Stones mock our mental ordering of time by reducing it
into a convergent instant that calls up memories of our early
ancestors who fixed their conscious will upon their stones.
And so rocks become the mnemonic aides for the unrav-
elling of this atavistic memory. They sign the paths to our

early psychic states. In the company of geology we can con-
nect with all the lives that came before us, and so the scryer
of geology is a commuter through the ancestral chains.

Geology provokes the mind to forgo its grip on time as a
thing falsely envisioned, frequently imprisoned, and so often
commodified. It returns to us a time of stateless liberty; a
Gaussian blur devoid of any fixity. When we gaze into a rock
we become as old as the earth itself. Figured stones, then,
are alms to break the capital's hegemony on temporality. The
scryer of geology gains a special *sensed perception* through a
prolonged reflection because any form of sustained interroga-
tion becomes a meditation upon the paradox of time.

Fleeting impressions held in rock, a hundred thousand
years of metamorphic resonance. In just a single stone all the
echelons were displayed before us; all true evidence of the
timeless gods were laid bare to see. The evidence is strong:
with enough time eventually everything will happen and only
geology will be its witness.

Author's Notes:

1   This may have a scientific basis, because iron oxide, which is contained in the bloodstone, is an effective astringent.

2   Refers to banded rhodochrosite which is mined in Argentina. It is also known as 'Rosa del Inca'.

3   Heliotrope translates to 'the turning of the sun'. The name came from the belief that when held in the rays of the setting sun, it would 'turn the sun' into a blood-red sphere. This ability of bloodstone to transform the sun's golden glow from gold to blood-red were attributed to its magical properties.

4   Bloodstone is also known as 'Chicken Blood Stone' in China.

5   Though the concept of geological *deep time* was proposed by the Scottish geologist James Hutton, the term itself was coined by the writer John Mcphee in his book *Basin and Range* (1981).

6   Up until his discovery the religious-centric world-view held that the age of the planet was a few thousand years old. Stratigraphic signatures and compositions of rock gave rise to Hutton's revised estimation of hundreds of millions years (still quite a way short of the current calculation of 4.54 billion years).

7   'The Idea of Labyrinth (Migong) in Chinese Building Tradition', Hui Zou, *The Journal of Aesthetic Education*, Vol. 46, No. 4 (Winter 2012), pp. 80–95.

8   Martin Heidegger, *Being and Time*, p, 377.

9   Curiously shaped and textured rocks traditionally appreciated and collected in China and Japan. Also known as scholar's rocks (see *Reliquiae* Volume 8 Number 1, pp. 25–37).

From Kwakiutl Folklore
Klawulacha / Song of the Totem-Pole

Waw haw le
Pulnakwila kiash ila koi
Wakiash kiash o wa
    Ya choi

Waw haw le
Hitlpalkwala kyilish
    Kiash ila koi
Kalakuyuwish kiash o wa
Lachnahkwulla
    Ya choi

Now doth it rise, our river;
Our river is Wakiash, good is he.

Now doth it creak, this totem-pole;
   Clouds rest on its top.
Kalakuyuwish, great as the sky-pole is he!

In praise of Wakiash Kalakuyuwish
Sung by Klalish

Note:

   The Kwakiutl are an Indigenous People who traditionally lived in what is now
   British Columbia, along the shores of the waterways between Vancouver Island
   and the mainland.

Taalawsohu

Morning Star, Venus

mamasawhòoyam

little death spirit

wukomunangw

great flow of water

hikwsi qa so'taniqa

eternal soul

Rebekah Clayton
yew

yew iwa eo iwen
from the graveyard
fecal-dropped

baccata red
coch dearg
gelatinous sweet

hard seeds disperse
feral evergreen
bitter alkaloids

lanceolate poison
nimh gwenwyn
bark hollow

hollow heartwood
Llangernyw cracked
sinuous age

old growing
growing iwen
eo iwa yew

Gaspar Orozco
El Libro de los Espejismos / The Book of Mirages (Excerpts)

1: *Hojas de un cuaderno Híkuri*

> *Para José Vicente Anaya*

Sobre nuestras cabezas, los cables de alta tensión zumban su plegaria negra. Aquí el portal de entrada. Murmullo de los números ciegos de la muerte.

Dejamos atrás la radiación al cruzar el lecho seco del arroyo.

*

Miel del desierto sobre la carne amarga del híkuri que se dejó encontrar por nosotros.

La generosidad del laberinto.

*

Soñamos puertas, puertas con signos de fuego.

Soñamos puertas.

*

1: *Pages from a Híkuri Journal*[1]

For José Vicente Anaya

Above our heads, the high tension wires buzz their black prayer. Here the entry portal. A murmuring of the blind numbers of death.

We leave the radiation behind, crossing the dry river bed.

   *

Desert honey on the bitter flesh of the peyote that allowed us to find it.

The generosity of the labyrinth.

   *

We dream doors, doors with signs of fire.

We dream doors.

   *

Vi una piedra con una gota de sangre de la tierra. La aparté y
la puse a mi lado para llevarla después conmigo. No la pude
encontrar. Quedó en algún lugar de la montaña.

Tengo que volver por ella.

*

Cuando volví a abrir los ojos, las piedras eran blancas, las
hierbas eran blancas, la tierra era blanca, la montaña era
blanca.

Sólo yo era oscuro.

*

El cielo tiembla con una vibración muy suave, una fragancia
muy tenue. El azul era un don fragilísimo e infinito.

*

Fuimos reyes sin más penumbra que la noche que
guardábamos en los ojos.

*

Una mariposa vino a posarse en mi rodilla izquierda. La
brisa de sus alas hizo reír al corazón, el amarillo de sus alas
encendió el árbol del alma.

*

I saw a stone with a drop of the earth's blood. I set it aside, placing it next to me to take later. I couldn't find it. It was left somewhere on the mountain.

I must return for it.

*

When I opened my eyes again, the stones were white, the grasses white, the earth was white, the mountain white.

Only I was dark.

*

The sky trembles with the slightest vibration, a faint fragrance. The blue was a most fragile and infinite gift.

*

We were royalty with no more shadow than the night we held in our eyes.

*

A butterfly came to rest on my left knee. The breeze of its wings kindled my heart, the yellow of its wings lit up the tree of my soul.

*

La música de los hombres se convierte en un ruido molesto frente a la música del desierto.

*

Los pájaros en los círculos abiertos del aire caliente.

Los humanos en los círculos abiertos del sueño.

En el valle, las sombras.

*

Desde la montaña alcanzo a ver las gruesas gotas de lluvia que comienzan a caer en mi casa de niño. Olor de tierra mojada, de nube que avanza sobre las piedras azules del camino. Un relámpago se alza en la distancia como la raíz blanca y diminuta de una hierba desconocida para mí.

*

El zumbido del moscardón es un oro purísimo.

*

La maravilla ante las flores silvestres que brillan en el viento seco y que no tienen nombre. Y entender que en el desierto, en la ladera de este monte donde las almas destellan en el aire ardiente, tampoco tenemos nombre.

*

The music of men becomes a jarring noise in the presence of
the desert's music.

*

Birds in the open circles of hot air.

Humans in the open circles of dreams.

In the valley, the shadows.

*

From the mountain I can see the thick rain drops that begin
to fall on my childhood home. The smell of damp earth,
of cloudcover closing in on the blue stones of the trail. A
distant bolt of lightning rises from the earth like the tiny,
white roots of an unknown grass.

*

The buzz of the blowfly is the purest of gold.

*

The marvel of wildflowers that shine in the dry wind and
have no name. And to understand the desert, on this side of
the mountain where souls glimmer in burning air, we, too,
are nameless.

*

Entre las capas del aire, vi el corazón del cielo. Se perdió de pronto entre los miles de pliegues del azul. Y el cielo siguió transmitiendo las ondas de su latido.

*

Sobre nuestras cabezas, los cables de alta tensión guardaron silencio al regreso. Y llega la noche en una estrella en la que arden todas las estrellas.

*

Descendimos de la montaña y emprendimos la vuelta al mundo.

Al lado de la carretera, un perro hambriento hundía su cabeza en una bolsa de plástico negra.

*

Between the layers of air, I saw the heart of the heavens. It was quickly lost among the thousands of folds of blue. The sky kept pulsing the waves of its own beat.

*

Above our heads, the high-tension wires remained silent upon our return. And the night comes as a star that burns with the flame of all the stars.

*

We descended the mountain, beginning our return to the world.

By the side of the road, a famished dog sunk his head into a black plastic bag.

*

Translator's Note:
   Híkuri is the Raramuri and Wixarica term for Peyote.

2

En las notas de sus viajes en México en la década de 1890,
Carl Lumholtz refiere que para los huicholes los cristales
de roca representaban *gente misteriosa, que al llamado del
shamán llegaban volando por el aire como pajaritos blancos,
que después se cristalizaban.* Tales cristales se guardaban
con celo, pues contenían el poder y la luz del alma de los
muertos, gente ejemplar de la tribu. Brindaban especial
poder en ese ritual tan importante para los huicholes,
la cacería del venado. *Los cazadores de venado* — escribe
Lumholtz — *se convierten en cristales al morir y acompañan
al sol en sus viajes. Viven donde el sol se alza, en un sitio
llamado 'donde las nubes se liberan a sí mismas'.*

2

In the notes from his travels through Mexico in the decade of the 1890s, Carl Lumholtz recounts that for the Huicholes, rock crystals represented *mysterious people, that at the shaman's call, arrived flying through the air like little white birds that would later crystallise.* Such crystals were jealously guarded, since they contained the power and the soul-light of the dead, exemplary people of the tribe. They provided special power in that ritual, so important for the Huicholes, the deer hunt. *The deer hunters —*writes Lumholtz*— become crystals upon dying and they accompany the sun in its journeys. They live where the sun rises, in a place called 'where the clouds set themselves free'.*

3

La sombra del pájaro a través de la hoja de la higuera. Lo que
dura un parpadeo, la silueta viva en ese traslúcido teatro.
Después, el temblor amarillo de la hoja vacía. La vi a través
del ventanal que daba al jardín interior. Un día de junio cuyo
único recuerdo es esta contraseña de la luz. Años después,
la dueña de la casa murió. La casa fue demolida y el jardín
destruido. Parte de la caída de una ciudad que no acaba de
cumplir su muerte para volver a nacer. No queda ahora sino
un terreno baldío, en donde el viento levanta remolinos de
polvo entre láminas y tablas. Imagino la muerte del vidrio
y de la hoja. Pero no puedo imaginar la muerte del pájaro
del que nunca vi sino la sombra, pájaro que para mí sigue
vivo, su corazón rojo latiendo en algún lugar del desierto,
proyectando su penumbra en la hoja amarilla de una higuera.

3

The shadow of a bird through a fig leaf. The duration of the
blink of an eye, the live silhouette in that translucent theatre.
After, the yellow tremor of an empty leaf. I saw it through
the picture window that opens onto the interior garden. One
June day whose only memory is this cipher of light. Years
later, the lady of the house died. The house was demolished
and the garden destroyed. Part of the decline of a city that
hasn't quite died in order to be born anew. There's nothing
left now but a barren plot, where the wind kicks up dust
devils between sheeting and boards. I imagine the death of
the glass and of the leaf. But I can't imagine the death of the
bird that I never saw but its shadow, a bird that still lives for
me, its red heart beating somewhere in the desert, projecting
its penumbra on the yellow leaf of a fig tree.

4

La telaraña estaba en lo alto del muro del jardín, extendida en la alambrada. Sin un hilo roto, su geometría—fiera y cerebral—ardía en cada punto y línea con el sol que se ponía en ese momento. En el centro, la emperatriz de ese palacio destellaba aún más, como un duro fragmento de ámbar suspendido. La duración de ese instante de descubrimiento y contemplación es imposible de medir. De pronto, un pájaro descendió sobre la tela y de un picotazo atrapó a la araña para alejarse aleteando en el aire de la tarde. La telaraña quedó vacía e inhabitada, un temblor en la luz de la hora. Nuestros ojos de niño no precisaban más para saber que el mundo nos había dejado al descubierto uno de sus silenciosos secretos. Ya tendríamos toda la vida para intentar desentrañarlo y volver, una y otra vez, al principio, a la telaraña que brilla una tarde en lo alto del muro del jardín.

4

The spider web hung at the top of the garden wall, stretched
across the barbed-wire. Without a single broken thread, its
geometry—fierce and cerebral—blazed, each point and line,
with the then-setting sun. In the centre, the empress of that
palace was shining even brighter, like a hardened fragment
of suspended amber. The duration of that exact moment
of discovery and contemplation is impossible to measure.
Suddenly, a bird swooped down on the web and in a single
beak-snap snatched the spider, only to wing itself off into the
distance of the afternoon air. The spider web was left empty
and bereft, a tremor in the light of that hour. Our child-
eyes needed no more to know that the world had revealed
one of its silent secrets to us. We would have the rest of our
lives to try and unravel it and return, over and over, to the
beginning, to the spider web that sparkles one afternoon at
the top of the garden wall.

Translated from Spanish by Ilana Luna

From Navajo Folklore
Dsichl Biyin / Mountain-Song

There are four worlds, one above the other: the first world;
the second world, which is the underworld; the third, which
is the middle world; and the fourth world, our own world. In
the underworld there arose a great flood and the people were
driven up by the waters. They planted a hollow reed and
came up through it to this world.

First-Man and First-Woman had brought with them earth
from the mountains of the world below. With this they made
the sacred mountains of the Navajo land.

To the East they placed the sacred mountain Sisnajinni.
They adorned it with white shell and fastened it to the earth
with a bolt of lightning. They covered it with a sheet of
daylight, and put the Dawn Youth and the Dawn Maiden to
dwell in it.

To the South they placed Tsodsichl. They adorned it with
turquoise and fastened it to the earth with a knife of stone.
They covered it with blue sky, and put the Turquoise Youth

and the Turquoise Maiden to dwell in it.

To the West they placed Doko-oslid. They adorned it with
haliotis-shell and fastened it to the earth with a sunbeam.
They covered it with a yellow cloud, and put the Twilight
Youth and the Haliotis Maiden to dwell in it.

To the North they placed Depenitsa. They adorned it with
cannel coal and fastened it to the earth with a rainbow.[1] They
covered it with a covering of darkness, and put the Youth of
Cannel Coal and the Darkness Maiden to dwell in it.

In the centre they placed Tsichlnaodichli and adorned it
with striped agate. Here were created the first Navajos. The
Navajos will never live elsewhere than around this mountain.

So the mountains were placed and decorated; then,
before they were named, holy songs were sung which tell of a
journey up the mountain. The song here given is the first of
these.

When the Navajo sings 'Chief of all mountains', he
means something higher and holier than chief. He sings
to the mountain as to a god, for the mountain is pure and
holy; there is freedom above it, freedom below it, freedom all
around it. Happiness and peace are given by the mountain,
and the mountain blesses man when in the song it calls him
'son'.

Dsichl Biyin

   Piki yo-ye!
Dsichl-nantaï,
   Piki yo-ye,
Sa-a naraï,
   Piki yo-ye,
Bike hozhoni,
   Piki yo-ye,
Tsoya shich ni-la!
   Piki yo-ye!

Mountain-Song

    Thither go I!
Chief of all mountains,
    Thither go I,
Living forever,
    Thither go I,
Blessings bestowing.
    Thither go I,
Calling me 'Son, my son.'
    Thither go I!

Notes:

    The Navajo are an Indigenous People of the South-western United States of America.

1   *Cannel coal,* a type of lustrous, bituminous coal.

Don Domanski
Two Poems

What the Bestiary Said

after many sorrows and thoughts broken
body pains and blows to the heart
after living in poorer lands
with human company in every mirror
I remembered what the bestiary said
and allowed the deer of the slender sadness
to take my voice and my hearing
the wolf of the impenetrable eyes
to remove my flesh and bone
the salmon to take my spirit
and I lay on lichens worn clean
by whispers close to the ground
so that I was the nothingness there
with only the beetle's breath to carry me till morning.

Transmigrational Poem (Garter Snake at Arisaig)

how often have we crawled
out of the amuletic
configurations of the grass

with glass teeth
and a gold-filling for a mind

how many times did we place
our invisible arms
around a heated day
as if it were an egg
warmed by a midden
of complexions
by a handful
of glittering scales.

iisaw

coyote

Maski

the underworld

muytala

moonlight

màasawnìwti

to be transformed into a death spirit

William Tyler Olcott
The Pleiades

> *Open those Pleiad eyes, liquid and tender,*
> *And let me lose myself among their depths.*
> — *De Vere*

No group of stars known to astronomy has excited such
universal attention as the little cluster of faint stars we know
as 'the Pleiades'. In all ages of the world's history they have
been admired and critically observed. Great temples have
been reared in their honour. Mighty nations have wor-
shipped them, and people far removed from each other have
been guided in their agricultural and commercial affairs by
the rising and setting of these close-set stars.

Many have been the metaphors inspired by this famous
cluster. They have been compared to a rosette of diamonds,
to a swarm of fireflies or bees, and the shining drops of dew.
Others have regarded these stars as a hen surrounded by
her chickens, and some have thought that they represented
the seven virgins. On the Euphrates the Pleiades and the
Hyades were known as 'the Great Twins of the Ecliptic'.
The Babylonians and Assyrians regarded them as a family
group without dreaming of the full significance of the title,

for modern science has proved that this group of suns have a common proper motion, that is, they are moving through space in the same direction, and are obviously part of one great system that holds them fast in bonds immutable.

The patriarch Job is thought to refer to the Pleiades in his word 'Kimah', meaning 'a cluster or heap', which occurs in the Biblical passages: '[God] maketh Arcturus, Orion, and the Pleiades and the Chambers of the South', and the familiar query: 'Canst thou bind the sweet influences of the Pleiades or loose the bands of Orion?' The meaning of this inquiry has been the cause of much conjecture and many attempts have been made to interpret the sense of it. E.W. Maunder thus explains the passage: when the constellations were first designed the Pleiades rose heliacally at the beginning of April and were the sign of the return of spring. Aratos wrote of them:

> Men mark their rising with the solar rays,
> The harbinger of Summer's brighter days.

The Pleiades which thus heralded the return of this genial season were poetically taken as representing the power and influence of spring. Their 'sweet influences' were those that rolled away the gravestone of snow and ice which had lain upon the winter tomb of nature. The question of Job was in effect, 'What control hast thou over the powers of nature? This is God's work, what canst thou do to hinder it?' Of the sweet influence of these fair stars we read again in Milton's *Paradise Lost*, where the poet sings of the Pleiades in the morning skies:

> ... the grey
> Dawn and the Pleiades before him danced,
> Shedding sweet influence.

In the *New Testament* we find the 'Seven Stars' also mentioned. In the first chapter of the Revelation, the Apostle St. John writes that 'he saw seven golden candle-sticks and in the midst of the seven candlesticks one like unto the Son of Man ... and He had in his right hand Seven Stars. The Seven Stars are of the angels of the seven churches, and the seven candlesticks are the seven churches.'

The Seven Stars in a simple compact cluster, says Maunder, stand for the church in its many diversities, and its essential unity. Modern almanacs designate the Pleiades 'the 7*' or 'seven stars'.

The Pleiades were among the first mentioned stars in the astronomical literature of China, one record of them bearing the early date of 2357 B.C., when Alcyone, the *lucida* of the group, was near the vernal equinox.

As might be expected, this celebrated group was the object of worship in Egypt. There the Pleiades were identified with the goddess Nit, meaning *the shuttle*, one of the principal divinities of Lower Egypt. The Great Pyramid, which was without doubt erected for astronomical purposes, is closely associated with the Pleiades, as Proctor has shown.

In the year 2170 B.C. the date at which the Pleiades really opened the spring season by their midnight culmination, they could be seen through the south passageway of this gigantic mausoleum. It has even been suggested that the seven chambers of the Great Pyramid commemorate these seven famous stars. Blake says: 'Either the whole of the conclusions respecting the pyramids is founded on pure imagination, or we have here another remarkable proof of the influence of the Pleiades on the reckoning of the year.'

The Arabians called the Pleiades, 'Atauria' signifying 'the little ones'. The Egyptians called this star group 'Athur-ai' or 'Atauria', meaning the stars of Athyr (Hathor), a name also given to the Seven Stars by the Chaldeans and Hebrews.

From this title is derived the Latin Taurus, and the German Thier. It is possible that this title was somehow connected with the Greek letter *tau*, and the sacred *scarabaeus* or tau beetle of Egypt. It has also been suggested that the 'tors' and Arthur's Seat, which were names given to British hilltops, may be connected with the 'high places' of the worship of the Pleiades. Arthur's Seat at Edinburgh is a notable example of such a site.

There appear to be three distinct derivations of the word Pleiades. First, from the Greek word πλέῖν, meaning 'to sail', the heliacal rising and setting of these stars marking the opening and closing of the season of navigation among the Greeks.

Second, from πέλειαι, meaning 'a flight of doves'. Hesiod, Pindar, and Simonides all use this word. The doves or pigeons were considered as flying from the mighty hunter Orion. They were also said to be the doves that carried ambrosia to the infant Zeus. D'Arcy Thompson asserts that the Pleiad is in many languages associated with bird names, and considers that the bird on the bull's back on coins of Eretria and Dicaea represents the Pleiades. We have a reduplication of this strange position of a bird among the constellational figures in the crow perched on the coils of Hydra.

A third derivation of the title of this group is from πλεῖος, meaning 'full' or in the plural 'many'. This derivation is considered to be the correct one by the weight of authority.

Many of the Greek temples were oriented to the Seven Stars, notably temples erected as early as 1530 and 1150 B.C., and the noted Parthenon built in 438 B.C. In the works of the Grecian poets we also find many references to the group.

Allen tells us that the Hindus pictured these stars as a flame typical of Agni, the god of fire, and regent of the asterism. The more usual representation of the group among the

Hindus was a razor; possibly the arrangement of the stars in the group suggested this title. It is thought that there may be a connection between the Hindu title 'Flame', and the great Feast of Lamps of the western Hindus held in the Pleiad season, October and November, a great festival of the dead which gave rise to the present Feast of Lanterns of Japan.

This closely associated star group has from time immemorial impressed humanity with a sense of mystery. A great cataclysm, possibly the Biblical Deluge, is in some way connected with the Pleiades, and some reference to such an event can be traced in many of the legends and myths surrounding these stars that have come down to us from nations far removed from each other.

Memorial services to the dead at the season of the year when the Pleiades occupied a conspicuous position in the heavens are found to have taken place, and to have been a feature in the history of almost every nation of the earth, from remote antiquity to the present day. The universality of this custom may well be considered one of the most remarkable facts that astronomical history records, and it serves to make the study of this group the most interesting chapter in all stellar history. This little group of stars, twinkling so timidly in the nights of autumn in the eastern heavens, links the races of humanity in closer relationship than any bonds save only nature's. No wonder that they have inspired universal awe and admiration—that within this group of suns we have sought to find the very centre of the universe.

Among the Aztecs of South America we find the Pleiades the cynosure of all eyes, a nation trembling at their feet. At the end of every period of fifty-two years, in the month of November when the Pleiades would culminate at midnight, the Aztecs imagined that the world would end. Human sacrifices were offered, while the entire population passed the night upon their knees awaiting their doom.

Far removed from the Aztecs we find the people of Japan in their great national festival, the Feast of Lanterns, a feast that is alive today, commemorating at this same season of the year some great calamity which was supposed to have overwhelmed the human race, in the far distant past, when these seven little stars were prominent in the heavens.

In the *Talmud* we find a curious legend associating the Pleiades with an all-destroying flood, expressed as follows: 'When the Holy One, blessed be He, wished to bring the deluge upon the world. He took two stars out of the Pleiades and thus let the deluge loose, and when He wished to arrest it, He took two stars out of Arcturus and stopped it.'

As we have seen, the ancient Hindus, the Aztecs, and the Japanese all had memorial festivals in the month of November. These generally occurred on the 17th of the month.

Among the ancient Egyptians the same day was observed, and although their calendar was subsequently changed, the occasion was not lost sight of. The date of their celebration was determined by the culmination of the Pleiades at midnight, and on this date the solemn three days' festival commenced. With them, as with the three previously mentioned nations, the festival was associated with the tradition of a deluge or humanity-destroying calamity. Blake says in regard to this that 'when we connect the fact that this festival occurred on the 17th day of Athyr, with the date on which the Mosaic account of the deluge of Noah states it to have commenced, in the second month of the Jewish year, which corresponds to November, the 17th day of the month, it must be acknowledged that this is no chance coincidence, and that the precise date here stated must have been regulated by the Pleiades, as was the Egyptian date.' Surely this is an interesting reference to the history of these stars.

The Persians formerly called the month of November 'Mordad', meaning 'the angel of death', and that month marked the date of their festival of the dead. On the 'day of the midnight culmination of the Pleiades, Nov. 17th, no petition was presented in vain to their ancient kings. In Ceylon, and in far distant Peru, a like festival took place at this season of the year. In the latter country the observation of the rising and setting of the Pleiades was the basis of their calendar.

The Society Islanders commenced their year on the first day of the appearance of the Pleiades, which occurred in November. This star group also marked a festival in commemoration of the dead which took place annually about the end of October in the Tonga Islands of the Fiji group.

Blake tells us that the first of November was with the ancient Druids of Britain a night full of mystery, in which they annually celebrated the reconstruction of the world. Although Druidism is now extinct the relics of it remain to this day, for in our calendar we still find Nov. 1st marked as 'All Saints' Day', and in the pre-Reformation calendar the last day of October was marked 'All Hallow Eve', and the 2nd of November as 'All Souls' Day', indicating clearly a three days' festival of the dead, commencing in the evening, and originally regulated by the Pleiades.

In France, the Parisians at this festival repair to the cemeteries and lunch at the graves of their ancestors. Prescott, in his *History of the Conquest of Mexico*, states that the great festival of the Mexican cycle was held in November at the time of the midnight culmination of the Pleiades, and the Spanish conquerors found in Mexico a tradition that the world was once destroyed when the Pleiades culminated at midnight, the identical tradition that we find in the far east, a myth so universal as to suggest a foundation of fact.

The actual observance at the present day of this festival is to be found among the Australian aboriginals. At the midnight culmination of the Pleiades, in November, they still hold a New Year's Corroboree in honour of this group of stars. The Corroborees are connected with a worship of the dead.

Many Masonic organisations of the present day have memorial services to the dead about the middle of November, a survival of the universal recognition of the season of the year as commemorating the destruction of the world, when the Pleiades culminated at midnight.

The fall of the year was especially appropriate as a season for memorial services for the dead, as nature's life was then at a low ebb and every prospect was suggestive of death, and the preparation for the long sleep imposed by winter. Thus we see in the association of this star group with this season of the year, a link that binds the remote past with the ever-living present in a most remarkable manner, and no one cognisant of these facts can watch these faintly glimmering stars with any feelings save those of awe and reverence.

Brown tells us that in the symbolism of Masonry the Pleiades play a prominent part. The emblem of the Seven Stars alludes to this star group as emblematic of the vernal equinox, thus making the Pleiades a beautiful symbol of immortality. It was for this reason that of all the 'hosts of heaven' the Pleiades were selected as an emblem.

In ancient times the appearance and disappearance of the Pleiades was associated with meteorological conditions. Statius calls them 'a snowy constellation'. Valerius Flaccus speaks of their danger to ships, and Horace pictures the south wind lashing the deep into storm in the presence of these famous stars. The Romans generally referred to the Pleiades as 'Vergiliae' or 'Virgins of Spring'. This star cluster was also of great service to the husband-man in marking the progress of the year. Hesiod thus alludes to the Pleiades:

There is a time when forty days they lie
And forty nights concealed from human eye,

> But in the course of the revolving year,
> When the swain sharps the scythe, again appear.

He also refers to the rising of the Pleiades as the time for the harvest, while the period at which they disappeared for some time, he termed ploughing time.

The heliacal rising of this star group, that is its rising with the sun, heralded the summer season, while its acronical rising, when it rose as the sun set, marked the beginning of winter, and led to the association of the group with the rainy season, and with floods, so often mentioned by the poets. Aratos thus expressed its acronical rising:

> Men mark their rising with Sol's setting light.
> Forerunners of the Winter's gloomy night.

Valerius Flaccus used the word 'Pliada' for showers, and Josephus tells us that during the siege of Jerusalem by Antiochus Epiphanes, in 170 B.C., the besieged wanted for water until relieved by a large shower of rain which fell at the setting of the Pleiades.

Pope in his 'Spring' thus alludes to the showery nature of the Pleiades:

> For see: the gath'ring flocks to shelter tend,
> And from the Pleiades fruitful showers descend.

Among the Dyaks of Borneo, the Pleiades regulated the seasons by their periodic return and disappearance, and guided them in their agricultural pursuits.

In South Africa, they were called the 'hoeing stars', and their last visible rising after sunset has been celebrated with rejoicing all over the southern hemisphere as betokening the summons to agricultural activity. Similarly, the Bantu tribe called the group 'the ploughing constellation'. With the Peruvians also the Pleiades governed the crops and harvest, and indeed were supposed to have created them.

Four thousand years ago this star group marked the position of the sun at the spring equinox, and this is the principal reason why, as we have seen, it was so universally associated with the apparent wax and wane of the forces of nature.

*

Many strange fables surround the Pleiades, quite apart and entirely disassociated with their classical mythology. The Pleiades was a favourite constellation of the Iroquois. In all their religious festivals the *calumet* was presented towards these stars, and prayers for happiness were addressed to them. They also believed that the Pleiades represented seven young persons who guarded the holy seed during the night.

An Onondaga legend concerning these stars is as follows: 'A long time ago a party of people journeyed through the woods in search of a good hunting ground. Having found one, they proceeded to build their lodges for the winter, while the children gathered together to dance and sing. While the children were thus engaged, an old man dressed in white feathers, whose white hair shone like silver, appeared among them and bid them cease dancing lest evil befall them, but the children danced on unmindful of the warning, and presently they observed that they were rising little by little into the air, and one exclaimed, "Do not look back for something strange is taking place." One of the children disobeyed this warning and looking back became a falling star. The other children reached the high heavens safely and now we see them in the star group known as the Pleiades.'

Another Native legend relates that 'seven brothers once upon a time took the warpath and discovered a beautiful maiden living all alone whom they adopted as their sister. One day they all went hunting save the youngest, who was left to guard his sister. Shortly after the departure of the hunters, the younger brother discovered game and set off in pursuit of it, leaving his sister unprotected. Whereupon a powerful buffalo came to her lodge and carried her away. The brothers returned and in dismay found that their sister had been taken from them. They immediately went in pursuit of her, only to find that she was confined in a lodge in the very centre of a great herd of fierce buffaloes. The younger brother cleverly tunnelled beneath them, however, and rescued his sister, and hastened homeward with her, where her brothers hedged her lodge about with a very high iron fence. The buffaloes, enraged at the escape of the maiden, attacked the seven brothers, and battered down the fence, only to find that the maiden and her brothers had been carried upward to the sky out of their reach, and there they may be seen in the cloistering Pleiades.'

The Shasta People of Oregon have the following legend concerning the Pleiades: 'The Coyote went to a dance with the Raccoon. On his return home he sent his children after the game he had killed, and when they had brought it in, he prepared a grand feast. The youngest child was left out, and in anger went to the Raccoon's children and told them that the Coyote had killed their father. The Raccoon's children revenged themselves by killing all the Coyote's children, save one, while the Coyote was away from home. They then disappeared. The Coyote, being unable to find his children, hunted everywhere, and asked all things as to their whereabouts. As he was searching he perceived a cloud of dust rising, and in the midst he saw the Raccoon's children and his youngest child. He ran after them in vain, and the children rose to the stars where they became the Pleiades.' The Coyote's child is represented by the faintest star of the group. In winter, when Raccoons are in their holes, the Pleiades are most brilliant, and continually visible. In summer, when Raccoons are out and about, the Pleiades are not to be seen.

The medicine men among the Malays, in their invocations, besought the Pleiades to help them heal bodily diseases. The Abipones, a tribe dwelling on the banks of the Paraguay River in South America, believed themselves descended from the Pleiades, and as that asterism disappeared at certain periods from the sky of South America, upon such occasions they supposed that their grandfather was sick, and were under a yearly apprehension that he was going to die, but as soon as the seven stars were again visible in the month of May, they welcomed their grandfather as if restored from sickness with joyful shouts and the festive sound of pipes and trumpets, and congratulated him on the recovery of his health. The hymn of welcome begins:

> What thanks do we owe thee?
> And art thou returned at last?
> Ah! thou hast happily recovered.

The Pleiades, according to classical mythology, were the seven daughters of Atlas, the giant who bears the world upon his shoulders, and the nymph Pleione. The story is that these seven maidens, together with their sisters the Hyades, were transformed into stars on account of their 'amiable virtues and mutual affection'. According to Aeschylus they were placed in the heavens on account of their filial sorrow at the burden imposed upon their father Atlas.

Aratos thus records the names of these seven sisters:

> These the seven names they bear:
> Alcyone and Merope, Celaeno,
> Taygeta, and Sterope, Electra,
> And queenly Maia, small alike and faint,
> But by the will of Jove illustrious all
> At morn and evening, since he makes them mark
> Summer and winter, harvesting and seed time.

One myth concerning the Pleiades relates that they were so beautiful in appearance that Orion unceasingly pursued them, much to their discomfiture. They appealed to Jupiter for assistance and he pitying them changed them into doves. Thereupon they flew into the sky and found a refuge among the stars.

The Smith Sound Inuit have the following legend concerning the Pleiades, which group they call 'Nanuq', meaning 'the Bear': 'A number of dogs were pursuing a bear on the ice. The bear gradually rose up in the air as did the dogs until they reached the sky. Then they turned to stars and the bear became a larger star in the centre of the group, and is represented by the star Alcyone.'

*

One of the seven stars in this cluster is not as brilliant as the others and this star the Greeks called 'the Lost Pleiad'. The tradition that one of the stars of this group has been lost or has grown dim is very ancient and almost universal. It is found among nations far removed from each other and has survived to the present day. It is found in Greece, Italy, and

Australia, among the Malays in Borneo, and the peoples of the Gold Coast. Byron thus alludes to this mysterious star:

Like the lost Pleiad seen no more below;

and Aratos wrote:

As seven their fame is on the tongues of men,
Though six alone are beaming on the eye.

There is little doubt that originally one of these stars was brighter than it now appears. Some of the Pleiades are known to be variable, and one of them may have lost lustre at some time far remote, a fact that may account for the tradition of a lost star.

It is interesting to review the myths and legends of the Lost Pleiad and the ingenious suggestions that have been made to account for its apparent loss of brilliancy.

As to which of the seven sisters disappeared mythology is uncertain. According to one story it was Electra, the mother of Dardanus, the founder of Troy, who hid her face in order that she might not see the destruction of that city. The Greeks claimed that the Lost Pleiad was Merope, who marrying a mortal, and feeling disgraced, withdrew from the company of her sisters. Some said the seventh Pleiad was struck by lightning, others that it was removed into the tail of the Great Bear. There is a myth that while a terrible battle was being waged on the earth, one of the sisters hid herself behind the others.

The Iroquois also had a legend respecting this famous star that appears to have been lost. They imagined that the Lost Pleiad was a little boy in the sky, who was very homesick. When he cried he covered his face with his hands and thus hid his light. The legend is as follows: 'Seven little boys lived in a log cabin in the woods, and every starlight night they joined hands and danced about singing the 'Song of the Stars'. The stars looked down and learned to love the children, and often beckoned to them. One night the children were very much disappointed with their supper, and so when they danced together and the stars beckoned to them, they accepted the invitation and betook themselves to Starland, and became the seven Pleiades, and the dim one represents one of the little boys who became homesick.'

Adapted for Reliquiae by the Editors

Jennifer Spector
Hithe (Excerpts)

Song for the Nightshade

a meadow
of seagrass   blue crab
Qi of the whale
land bidding
samphire & aquatic fern
        speedwell   salmon   manatee
foxgloves awaiting bloom

bells straying the prairie
thrum ianthine nightshade

echo over the machair
lifting helmet of kelp
& sand   pillowing bent
tussocks   waterforms
oxygen at root

continents tilting the cold

sibylline river courting
the deserted hour
draped in sea-score
& churn of rare flower

shade of sorrel hair whorling
what has brought you here
across the wide arms of the sea?

here, shelter   / here a crest
O breathe the broken letters
how they choke the throat

a spray of order
green of fading song
song fading through body
body passing through the world

what have we
left to suede this
place of shadow?

                    old leaning
            without name
making for the old tangles

A Little Way

at Los Cayos Holandeses, Guna Yala, Panamá

September's cast
      to the corals   only six ft deep

little fruit has plundered reason
      corners tucked non-geometrically

   come around
      the hatches are opened
the berth is good
      angelfish scatter the keel in
vesture of half-light

   tacking   we watch for wind
      his purled sweep to the bars
where he settles

here for tonight   wooing the white-ruffed manakins
scarlet tanagers and woodcreepers   on slender breach

spelling the course
    we have augury's summer   tying the hawthorns
plump figs and sweet haw and Thalia's port
                ripe cheese lodging in wine

    steady the gooseneck & lane   as sun downs
against a plaza of mangroves

Tsöötsöqam

Pleiades

tunatyawtaqa

guardian spirit

kwaahu

golden eagle

masavuyàlti

to spread the wings

Frances Horovitz
Four Poems

West Kennet Long Barrow

enter the throat of darkness
follow the word
      winding to the heart of the stone
the dead welcome you
listen, their skulls echo with silence
          their bones sing
they have trodden the long path
          to the threshold of light
they burn with the star and the stone
they are one with the bird and the wind

Elegy for the Mummy of a Young Girl in the British Museum

Cleopatra,
daughter of Candace
of Western Thebes,
in the second month
of her twelfth year,
stopped her breathing
—the papyrus does not say
what date or season.

Dried berry beads scattered in the hot sand,
blue and white dress by the river,
white flowers in your hair.

73

Buried with the Book of Breathings
at your head and foot
(spells to propitiate
those crocodile and jackal heads)
and instructions for
Traversing Eternity,
you leave behind
your faded flowers,
the wooden comb
and string of berry beads.
The painted sky goddess leans down
to take you in her arms.
What birds fly with you,
ibis or swallow,
we do not know
nor how light the feather
to weigh against your heart.

Quanterness, Orkney 3500 B.C.

Not blood, but fact, from stones and the sieved dust.

'Most die at twenty'
                         —syllables snatched by wind.
Died of bone's ache, belly's ache,
                     the ninth shining wave,
or long attrition of the absent sun.
'Before the Pyramids, this death-house
was the centre of their lives.'
Equal in death,
man, woman, young and old,
laid out for carrion, their wind-scoured bones
heaped hugger-mugger in the corbelled dark.
'Some rodent bones were also found.'

Each desperate spring
winds drift flower-scent from off the sea;
lambs call like children.
In warm heather
the young lie breast to breast
seeding the brief sun into their flesh.

Womb-hunger to outlast the stones.

Poem found at Chesters Museum, Hadrian's Wall

To Jove, best and greatest
and to the other immortal gods;
to Augustus, happy and unconquered
Victory, holding a palm branch;
to Hadrian
commemorating 343 paces of the Roman Wall

> *bill hook, holdfast, trivet*
> *latch lifter, nail lifter, snaffle bit*
> *sickle blade, terret ring, spear butt*
> *boat book, entrenching tool*
> *chisel, gouge, gimlet, punch*

To Longinus, trumpeter
and Milenus, standard bearer
1st Cohort of the Batavians;
to Cornelius Victor
served in the army 26 years
lived 55 years 11 days
erected by his wife;
to Brigomaglos, a Christian;
to my wife Aelia Comindus
who died aged 32

unguentaria
balsamaria
ivory comb
pins of bronze and bone
dress fastener
strap fastener
spinning whorls
needles, spoons
Millefiori beads
ligula, earprobe
tongs

To the woodland god Cocidius;
to Coventina, water goddess
and attendant nymphs

 —in her well
 axe hammer
 spiral ring, jet ring
 dogbrooch, coins

To the Mother Goddesses
to the gods of this place
to the goddesses across the water
to the old gods
to a god ...

dedication partly obliterated
with human figure in rude relief
text of doubtful meaning
dedication illegible

uninscribed

stone of ...

Rebecca Drake
Awntyrs, women (Excerpt)

I: *At the shore—*

'Whider scholde ich wimman bringe?
I ne have none kines thinge.
I ne have hus, I ne have cote,
I ne have sticke, I ne have sprote,
I ne have neither bred ne sowel,
Ne cloth, but of an old white covel.'

Did she not pray for the bower doors to fall
open? Did she not long to leap
past the causeway into the sea

adrift? This is not the life she had in mind—
bound to a withered willow of a boy, locked,
mired to his knees in mud, blood, fish guts.

Has he not brought her treasures?
Unseeing pearls of oyster shells.
A bed frame of driftwood. A mattress of seaweed.

Salt fish that sparkle in chests like diamonds.
A seal-strung harp. A whale bone comb to rake
the ocean tresses of her hair. Strings

of sapphire scales interlocked like marsh channels
scalloped by darting sandpiper wings.
He has learned to wrestle fen, to breathe eel-like, lungs

weighing mud to bring her feasts for a king.
But he is hooked by the gills to their table,
mucus writhing, long limbs wracked

in spasms as the burning tide
turns hungry towards land
red-flecked while Goldboru waits

at the foreshore, awaits
a boat, a sail, a wing
a dream of winging *over the se.*

Author's Notes:

  The title uses a Middle English spelling of 'adventure' and refers to the romance,
  The Awntyrs off Arthure.

  'Whider scholde ich wimman bringe?', lines 1139–1144 of the Middle English
  romance, *Havelok the Dane.*

Isidro Li
Four Poems

Rio de Montaigne

In these hours,
how true is north?

A river is intent
on approaching.

When is it not
this matter of place, this why?

Don't ask: should we all be lit
from within? To question

is to measure a hymn by a circle.
But from the rim of this other world

I chance no grief, no tear of the clouds.
Knowing it is difficult. Knowing enough

to harness the power of water. But to care
for the unseen roots of self.

As flame is to mouth, we let the blessed in.
And they remain.

Excerpt from the Book of Waves and Fossils

who owns bones
bones do own

even the tide
an understory

vast and Neolithic
a being of blue

mist we evolve
and gift it a name

where sentience
is isthmus

argosies sail
unseen

time scales
the eyes

and music
is actuality

is of
this world

Nectere

salt not of this earth
a pair of tiny shoes

by the door a minus
sign of a distant tidal

lock and key to this language
of having asked for so little

I want nothing
but the extract

a memory of often
this evening star

and tomorrow
blood oranges
sudden dew

Solve et Coagula

there is now
the power in us

to be ondful
to be as it were

hold it in your hands
it won't bite

this tiny rabbit heart
this white lung of winter

a table alphabetic
of tall grasses

brooding galaxies
the pluck of the seas

o sad black faces
o landed gentry

I just want to be left alone
there is so much to ask for

From The Tanner Bede
Caedmon's Hymn

Nu sculon herigean heofonrices weard,
meotodes meahte and his modgeþanc,
weorc wuldorfæder, swa he wundra gehwæs,
ece drihten, or onstealde.

He ærest sceop eorðan bearnum
heofon to hrofe, halig scyppend;
þa middangeard moncynnes weard,
ece drihten, æfter teode
firum foldan, frea ælmihtig.

Praise the ward of the kingdom of heaven,
the might of the maker and the mind's undertaking,
the father in glory, the Lord everlasting, the work when he
outset the onrush of wonders.
First did he fashion the roof of high heaven for all of earth's
    children —
master almighty and holy creator, the ward of all people and
for all the people he afterwards clad in rich earth the whole
    world,
the Lord everlasting.

Translated from West Saxon by Peter O'Leary

Translator's Note:
    Manuscript source: MS Tanner 10, Oxford, Bodleian Library.

Frater Acher
The Straight Line is a Trap

Nature abhors a vacuum, the biologist knows from research.
Nature eschews a straight line, the magician would add from
life experience. Even the horizon bows. Each stem bends.
Every crystal's line ultimately breaks in a sharp edge. While
everything in nature is filled with purpose, nothing pursues
that purpose in a straight line. The meandering path of a
river is not a detour or diversion from its desire to unite with
the ocean. Quite the opposite: the curve is a river's way of
speaking mildly to everything it encounters on its path. A
rivulet curls around stones, a stream leans against moun-
tains, and the vessel of a lake offers a moment of rest.

Once we let go of the straight line as the singular mode
of travel in the industrialised age, as if through magic, all
obstacles cease to exist. My holy daïmon once told me: *When
there is no defence, there also is no attack.* While this koan
might not hold true in warfare tactics, it presents wonderful
food for thought for our everyday lives. Especially when we

are engaging in magic.

Since the time of the Ancient Egyptians, magic was known to be a craft and art of crisis intervention. Whether these were personal crises of spiritual or bodily health, or calamities relating to the land that supported an entire people, magic was looked upon as the *secret discipline*—half occult armoury, half medicine chest—that held recipes against all forms of disaster. In this vein, magic was often thought of as the exact antithesis to the volatile, unpredictable ways of the gods and natural forces. Magic was expected, especially by the laity, to be the straightest of all lines, the shortest route from chaos to order, from vulnerability to safety.

Few people trouble themselves with a reputation that exceeds actual reality. If the old adage 'perception is reality' plays in their favour, most people don't worry to correct it. They simply enjoy the benefits of their inflated esteem until the very moment when the litmus test arrives, and they are standing in front of a sick king not knowing what to do, or in front of an approaching sandstorm with all but a candle and an empty prayer on their lips.

The truth is, magic can indeed be leveraged as a means of crisis prevention. However, such magic relies on communion with spirits and other-than-human intelligences, precisely for the purposes of understanding how the trap that is the straight line might best be avoided. One of the most basic and yet critical realisations on the magical path is that the price for the potion that mixes free will with magical power comes at the burden of bearing all sorts of consequences. The more the magician attempts to affect change, to intervene in the organic interplay of myriads of living ecosystems, the more they must be ready to own the impact of that intervention in all its facets. Many magical acts, even early on in one's path, can be compared to releasing an arrow from a bowstring: they are deceptively simple, and in most cases they will hit *something*. Yet the problems begin when that *something* is not at all what we intended to hit. For there is no such thing as taking back an arrow released from a bow.

The famous occult novelist Gustav Meyrink (1868–1932) hinted at the perilous nature of the magical act in his 1927 novel on the magical life of John Dee:

> *The rabbi just smiles with his eyes.*
> *'You goyim can shoot with the crossbow and with the rifle. A wonder how you aim and hit! An art, how you shoot! But can you also pray? A wonder how you aim wrong and how seldom you ... hit!'*
> *'Rabbi! A prayer is not a bullet from a barrel!'*
> *'Why not, your honour? A prayer is an arrow in God's ear! If the arrow hits, the prayer is answered. Every prayer is answered, – must be answered, for prayer is irresistible, ... if it hits.'*
> *'And if it does not hit?'*
> *'Then the prayer falls down again like a lost arrow, sometimes it hits something by accident, falls to the earth like Onan's power – or ... it is intercepted by the Other and his servants. They then answer the prayer in ... their way!'*
> *'From which 'other'?' I ask with fear in my heart.*

(Gustav Meyrink, *Der Engel vom Westlichen Fenster*, 1927, p. 312, translated for this essay by the author)

As a magical novitiate there is no reason to be concerned about the 'Other' – as long as we don't wander in foreign lands shooting arrows, until we have become one with the terrain, as well as with the bow that holds our arrow. Unfortunately, this advice is not at all meant metaphorically. For, in magic, the straight line that presents the trap *is the ritual itself*.

Now, this is where the study of classical magical texts, such as medieval grimoires or the Greek Magical Papyri, becomes fascinating. Strip away the actual ritual act, efface anything thrown in to satisfy the reader's appetite for pomp, power or performance, and observe what remains.

To some modern readers it might sound paradoxical to scrutinise a text of ritual magic for everything except the ritual itself, but such confusion is easily resolved once we learn what magic truly comprises. To understand the nature of a river, we wouldn't seek the place of its source and then go straight to the point where it flows into the sea. Even looking up its direction and its sinuous forms on a map would not suffice to understand its nature. To truly learn about a river, we have to walk for miles along its bank, to row and drift on its water. Or we must live close by its waterside for many years, sitting occasionally on its bank, listening. Neither action, nor even the ability to 'cause change to occur in conformity with one's will' (Aleister Crowley), present the most precious outcome in the occult arts. But *understanding* does. Our ability to attune ourselves, to see and sense from within, not only into a single environment or spirit being, but into myriads of them. One at a time, remaining agile and light-footed, yet calm and concentrated on each step of the path. Becoming easy like air, fluid like water, fast like fire and yet detached like a stone, these are the qualities of the magical adept. And none are gained by travelling in a straight line.

Many years ago, I was about to embark on a magical operation that continues to this day. As so often with men, especially young men, I had lofty goals for myself and the impact my magic should create. I aimed not at personal gain, but at helping the land I lived on to become free from the patterns of its past. Still, here I was: a lone practitioner against decades of magical patterning, repeated by thousands, if not millions, of people. As it held the promise of healing the world, it was the kind of arrow to shoot from my bow that is most tempting for adolescent men. *Much enemy, much ore,* as they say. Luckily, before I went ahead with a plan I had carefully devised over months—and after more than a decade of magical training—I asked a wise woman, Josephine McCarthy, for counsel. She interrupted me a few sentences into the description of my master plan, and advised that this was a perfect plan if I intended to annihilate myself. She then gave me a lesson that changed not only my magical, but also my everyday, life: *If you intend to create change of significance, don't walk into the eye of the storm, but work from its periphery.*

If we returned to Meyrink's occult novel, the white rabbi might have suggested that learning how to pray was analogous to the way we listen to birds, to the wind in the oat grass, or to the murmuring of water, rather than to the shooting of a crossbow or rifle. Knowing *how* to pray, without falling prey to the 'Other', becomes the easiest of skills, once we have learned how to listen.

I suspect that many of us still know this. Those of us who sit still in meditation; who go out into the forest at dusk and return at dawn; who find a remote place to retreat to in silence; who spread out ashes on the floor and lie down among them. Those of us who know how to lock the door and find comfort in our cell. Many of us still know this, I dare to hope: that our body is the *athanor* of the craft, and that it is through our heart-space that the fire comes, just as it is the periphery of our body where magic takes place.

*

Before I close, allow me to share a most simple exercise to explore this premise yourself: sit down in a sufficiently quiet, dark room and light a candle. Put it in front of you on the floor, about four feet away, and stare into it unblinkingly for as long as you can. Take your time; try over a couple of days until you reach five to ten minutes of a single stare without needing to blink. Allow your eyes to go teary, it will do you no harm. Just continue staring into the flame. Then—after a few weeks of practice—light a second candle. Now move both flames to the periphery of your vision; one left, one right. Shift them out as far as you can; just make sure you can still see the centres of the flames if you turn your eyes hard. Then lower your stare straight ahead again and try to see both flames at once in the periphery of your vision.

This technique is called *tratak* and the two exercises shared above will teach you to assume 'single-minded vision' as well as '180 degree vision'. Now, did you fall into the trap? Of course, the technique is important as it stands. It teaches your body and creates a specific sensual experience. It changes your eyes, your vision, your mind, your breath and your brain, and many other things. But *tratak* itself is not magic. You might encounter the latter as soon as you stop trying to achieve something with this exercise—and yet, keep going. You might encounter magic once you cease caring about the flames, once you cease caring about your vision or what you might see or not see. Because, in such moments, there is no longer any centre and neither is there periphery. All that remains, in these short seconds, is the experience. The hearing of the present moment. It is in moments like these that we can walk over trapdoors without falling.

For many of us it takes decades of practice to realise this simple truth: magic doesn't sleep in the chalice. Magic doesn't sleep in the wand, the sword, the circle or the sigil. It sleeps within the periphery of our own bodies. That is where it is rooted. On that razor thin edge, where we end and another begins.

uuwingw

the element of fire

paatalawva

to begin to shimmer with rainwater

qatungwu

form that held life, stalk, corpse

wimtawi

ritual song

Triin Paja
Four Poems

The Wrong Myth

if you're metamorphosed into the atmosphere, then the
birds will carry you here, writhing across water in wings and
barnacled fishing boats, in a gossamer nothing of salt, wind,
famine.

everything I touch belongs to the dead. you have drunk,
drowned, and birthed me. my particles have already loved
you in a weed-buried century. on another day, I birthed dead
animals. I was a bird whose egg would not, like light, crack.
still I waited and nurtured.

an egg without a pulse remains a memory of the sky. a
featherless, elliptical lake of protein. Pegasus budded from
the puddle of his mother's blood. meaning the tremors of
beauty are also the tremors of terror.

I wanted to speak of you in limestone, dead volcanoes,
and blue. what can I say? an old woman reached from her
apartment window to feed pigeons. you would think this
loneliness lovely. we have also turned to birds, wanting to be
delicately touched.

I know we must give the dead a window, for even the
earthworms grow gangrenous, but this is the wrong myth.
the wrong side. you are also waiting for the birds to carry us
to you.

Daughters

I knew an old, lonely girl
whose doll was a moose bone.

she laid against
ravelled raven-dark roots,

in the hollows left by deer,
and carried back her own blossoming.

in the house,
pearling still meant perishing.

in the house, bread was broken
and then bodies.

her spruce-wild voice
was mangled into sweetness.

in the house, the sun was a rotting apricot.
beyond the house, the sun

was generous and she ate
the crumbs of the sun like the birds,

saying *father, father.*

her body unfurled only beyond visibility,
and so the forest became

her resting place, her bones became
dolls for bears and otters.

later, I heard her father say:
I always loved daughters more than sons—

how he cried for two years, every day,
after her passing. how he opens

his small, yellow bible, and disappears.

A Portrait of Old Animals

I

I carve a cross for a bird's grave
while the cold wind sings terrible songs

into the ears of feral kittens.
I believed the wind was the wingspan

of a ghost, but it is only the wind,
the way the earth is only earth.

I recall my first bird, a kaleidoscopic bird,
an anarchy of light. then someone said

bird, and the bird attained its birdness.
afterwards, it was impossible to see them.

II

on this earth, I entered a forest
and crushed a clover with my breathing.

on this earth, a man collects the frozen feet
of elephants and another fills his freezer

with tiger cubs. on this earth, I see a grave
in each beetle-ghosted rose

and never see the bird, the elephant,
the tiger. over the forest floor,

twigs fall in the shape of crosses.

Winter Farm

the way to the farm,
the glow of the frozen path,

then calves, forked
swallow tails, hay rot.

her hay-wounded hands.
dead bee-light in the milk-

powdered corridor.
to know the axe silvering

into frozen hay stacks.

to know a mother's pain:
a child carrying a lamb

in her lap, a child building
a shelter of birch twigs.

she named the bones
in the slaughter house,

each of the hundreds of animals
had a name. we brushed our hands

over their rose tongues.

in the half-limbed light
of the winter farm,

the rattle of chains.

From Navajo Folklore
Dsichl Biyin / Mountain-Song

I

    Be-ye-la-naseya,
    Be-ye-la-naseyo,
    Be-ye-la-naseya,
Ho-digin-ladji-ye-ye,
    Be-ye-la-naseya,
Ka' Sisnajinni
  Bine dji-ye-ye,
    Be-ye-la-naseya,
Dsichl-nanitaï
  Bine dji-ye-ye,
    Be-ye-la-naseya,
Sa-a naraï
  Bine dji-ye-ye,
    Be-ye-la-naseya,
Bike hozhoni
  Bine dji-ye-ye,
    Be-ye-la-naseya.

I

    Swift and far I journey,
    Swift upon the rainbow;
    Swift and far I journey.
Lo, yonder, the Holy Place!
    Yea, swift and far I journey.
To Sisnajinni, and beyond it,
    Yea, swift and far I journey;
The Chief of Mountains, and beyond it,
    Yea, swift and far I journey;
To Life Unending, and beyond it,
    Yea, swift and far I journey;
To Joy Unchanging, and beyond it,
    Yea, swift and far I journey.

II

Be-ye-la-nadesta,
Be-ye-la-naseyo,
Be-ye-la-nadesta,
Ho-digin-ladji-ye-ye,
Be-ye-la-nadesta,
Ka' Sisnajinni
Bine dji-ye-ye,
Be-ye-la-nadesta,
Dsichl-nanitaï
Bine dji-ye-ye,
Be-ye-la-nadesta,
Sa-a naraï
Bine dji-ye-ye,
Be-ye-la-nadesta,
Bike hozhoni
Bine dji-ye-ye,
Be-ye-la-nadesta.

II

Homeward now shall I journey,
Homeward upon the rainbow;
Homeward now shall I journey.
Lo, yonder, the Holy Place!
    Yea, homeward now shall I journey.
To Sisnajinni, and beyond it,
    Yea, homeward now shall I journey;
The Chief of Mountains, and beyond it,
    Yea, homeward now shall I journey;
To Life Unending, and beyond it,
    Yea, homeward now shall I journey;
To Joy Unchanging, and beyond it,
    Yea, homeward now shall I journey.

III

    Be-ye-la-nikiniya,
    Be-ye-la-naseyo,
    Be-ye-la-nikiniya,
Ho-digin-ladji-ye-ye,
    Be-ye-la-nikiniya,
Ka' Sisnajinni
  Bine dji-ye-ye,
    Be-ye-la-nikiniya,
Dsichl-nanitaï
  Bine dji-ye-ye,
    Be-ye-la-nikiniya,
Sa-a naraï
  Bine dji-ye-ye,
    Be-ye-la-nikiniya,
Bike hozhoni
  Bine dji-ye-ye,
    Be-ye-la-nikiniya.

III

    Homeward behold me starting,
    Homeward upon the rainbow;
    Homeward behold me starting.
Lo, yonder, the Holy Place!
    Yea, homeward behold me starting.
To Sisnajinni, and beyond it,
    Yea, homeward behold me starting;
The Chief of Mountains, and beyond it,
    Yea, homeward behold me starting;
To Life Unending, and beyond it,
    Yea, homeward behold me starting;
To Joy Unchanging, and beyond it,
    Yea, homeward behold me starting.

IV

Be-ye-la-naïshtatl,
Be-ye-la-naseyo,
Be-ye-la-naïshtatl,
Ho-digin-ladji-ye-ye,
Be-ye-la-naïshtatl,
Ka' Sisnajinni
  Bine dji-ye-ye,
    Be-ye-la-naïshtatl,
Dsichl-nanitaï
  Bine dji-ye-ye,
    Be-ye-la-naïshtatl,
Sa-a naraï
  Bine dji-ye-ye,
    Be-ye-la-naïshtatl,
Bike hozhoni
  Bine dji-ye-ye,
    Be-ye-la-naïshtatl.

IV

    Homeward behold me faring,
    Homeward upon the rainbow;
    Homeward behold me faring.
Lo, yonder, the Holy Place!
    Yea, homeward behold me faring.
To Sisnajinni, and beyond it,
    Yea, homeward behold me faring;
The Chief of Mountains, and beyond it,
    Yea, homeward behold me faring;
To Life Unending, and beyond it,
    Yea, homeward behold me faring;
To Joy Unchanging, and beyond it,
    Yea, homeward behold me faring.

V

Be-ye-la-nanistsa,
Be-ye-la-naseyo,
Be-ye-la-nanistsa,
Ho-digin-ladji-ye-ye,
Be-ye-la-nanistsa,
Ka' Sisnajinni
Bine dji-ye-ye,
Be-ye-la-nanistsa,
Dsichl-nanitaï
Bine dji-ye-ye,
Be-ye-la-nanistsa,
Sa-a naraï
Bine dji-ye-ye,
Be-ye-la-nanistsa,
Bike hozhoni
Bine dji-ye-ye,
Be-ye-la-nanistsa.

V

    Now arrived home behold me,
    Now arrived on the rainbow;
    Now arrived home behold me.
Lo, here, the Holy Place!
    Yea, now arrived home behold me.
At Sisnajinni, and beyond it,
    Yea, now arrived home behold me;
The Chief of Mountains, and beyond it,
    Yea, now arrived home behold me;
In Life Unending, and beyond it,
    Yea, now arrived home behold me;
In Joy Unchanging, and beyond it,
    Yea, now arrived home behold me.

VI

Be-ye-la-nanishta,
Be-ye-la-naseyo,
Be-ye-la-nanishta,
Ho-digin-ladji-ye-ye,
Be-ye-la-nanishta,
Ka' Sisnajinni
Bine dji-ye-ye,
Be-ye-la-nanishta,
Dsichl-nanitaï
Bine dji-ye-ye,
Be-ye-la-nanishta,
Sa-a naraï
Bine dji-ye-ye,
Be-ye-la-nanishta,
Bike hozhoni
Bine dji-ye-ye,
Be-ye-la-nanishta.

VI

Seated at home behold me,
Seated amid the rainbow;
Seated at home behold me.
Lo, here, the Holy Place!
Yea, seated at home behold me.
At Sisnajinni, and beyond it,
Yea, seated at home behold me;
The Chief of Mountains, and beyond it,
Yea, seated at home behold me;
In Life Unending, and beyond it,
Yea, seated at home behold me;
In Joy Unchanging, and beyond it,
Yea, seated at home behold me.

Note:

Each song is sung four times. In each subsequent repetition, Sisnajinni is replaced with the names of the mountains Tsodsichl, Doko-oslid and Depenitsa.

Shash Trevett
Waratah

Sydney, 1787

She clutched her collection of words
bulbous, tightly packed, ageless
like the flame heads of the Waratah
burning skywards along the songlines
of the Eoran people.

Bógee — to bath or to swim
Nánga — to sleep, *Patá* — to eat,
Naa — to see, *Ŋyínadyımíŋa* —
You stand between me and the fire.

In Dreamtime the Waratah bloomed white
until an encounter between a hawk
and a wonga pigeon above it
turned the white flower red.

Red seeds, red words. From her hands to his
passed perfectly formed capsules of time
and memory. A florescence
of a crimson, breathing language.

Dteéwara – hair, *NGára* – to hear.
Catching fish on a hook made from bark.
Putuwá, she said. 'I warm my hand
by the fire and then gently
squeeze your hand in mine'.

When he sailed home he carried with him
her voice compact in his notebooks
and a single Waratah head.
Gwára buráwá – The wind is falling, she said.
Búŋabaoú buk ŋyɪniwágolàŋ
I will make a book for you, he replied.

Author's Note:

In 1787, Patyegarang, a young girl from the Eoran tribe, who inhabited the area which would become Sydney, taught the Eoran language to William Dawes, a young English botanist and engineer. The Eorans were soon wiped out by small-pox and European colonialism. The word 'Waratah' comes from the Eoran, and the only record of the language survives in the notebooks Dawes kept of his time with Patyegarang.

angwusi

raven

qöqòönaqa

fire tender

katsina

a spirit being

qe"iwma

abating, subsiding

Don Domanski
Pleiades

I was walking back barefooted
I was walking back to you
on the night I was born

there was a rust-coloured moon over my head
a sun-turned moon
changing the road into metal
into blue foil

to the left a black rain was falling
to the right a shower of gold was dissolving
a field of white stones
in front of me I carried gifts for you
in one outstretched hand
I held a bent nail
in the other a moth
they were the only suitable things
worth bringing into the world

on that night I could
think of nothing
I walked up a street
and walked back down it again

when I turned
my coat turned with me
to hear the wind
the voices driven past the moon
past the dull green leaves
on the half-finished tree

I felt small as a leaf
like the ghost of a hand
hem of a centipede
discarded inside a white cup

I placed a hand in my pocket
and felt the ocean moving
through my clothes
the fish   the round stones
the eight varieties of seaweed
common to this area

I took my new name
out of my pocket
and read it over once again

while up there
just above the rooftops
the moon and the wind
and seven dead girls
sitting on six burning chairs
spun slowly by

and with fourteen gloved hands
they were all pointing to you.

Penelope Shuttle
the half-guest

brings his heart
sinewy & very gentle
brings gold-gifts of treasure
for marriages made continually at night
brings the magnetic thirst of stars
fierce swan of the tundra
goblet of the silkworm

in the amber council of good fortune
the half-guest speaks
a prayer day of sea-horse runes
says our sins
are pearls and rubies
blesses us with what we crave
seclusion from wolf-craft

Robin Walter
Six Poems

Pray not to behold

but to be held by

Meadow cupped by bowl of blue sky,
wind rivering quiet

then quick
through lodgepole pines —

Small reverie

of nest,

If I could make
of myself so true

a shelter, palms
pressed

—Vein

of yellow
aspens

splits
the mountain

dark—

—At the edge

of the pine,
a little snow

lifts

—Across snow,

winter shadows
deepen—

—Longing
to be a nest,

the hand
folds open

at night—

Mercy of meadow

covered
in snow,

fleck
of mica

edged
in granite

offers
the quarter-

moon
back to itself—

*

In the morning,
light rivers

the body
edged

in water—

wide nest
of palm

cradles
the river-

rinsed
face—

Donald A. Mackenzie
Babylonian and Egyptian Astronomy (Excerpt)

Beliefs regarding the stars were of similar character in
various parts of the world. But the importance which they
assumed in local mythologies depended in the first place
on local phenomena. On the northern Eur-Asian steppes,
for instance, where stars vanished during summer's blue
nights, and were often obscured by clouds in winter, they
did not impress men's minds so persistently and deeply as
in Babylonia, where for the greater part of the year they
gleamed in darkness through a dry transparent atmosphere
with awesome intensity.

In various countries all round the globe the belief pre-
vailed that the stars were ghosts of the mighty dead – of
giants, kings, or princes, or of princesses, or of pious people
whom the gods loved, or of animals which were worshipped.
A few instances may be selected at random. When the
Teutonic gods slew the giant Thjasse, he appeared in the
heavens as Sirius. In India the ghosts of the 'seven Rishis',

who were semi-divine Patriarchs, formed the constellation
of the Great Bear, which in Vedic times was called the 'seven
bears'. The wives of the seven Rishis were the stars of the
Pleiades. In Greece the Pleiades were the ghosts of the seven
daughters of Atlas and Pleione, and in Australia they were
and are a queen and six handmaidens.

The Arcadians believed that they were descended, as
Hesiod recorded, from a princess who was transformed by
Zeus into a bear; in this form Artemis slew her and she
became the 'Great Bear' of the sky. The Egyptian Isis was
the star Sirius, whose rising coincided with the beginning
of the Nile inundation. Her first tear for the dead Osiris fell
into the river on 'the night of the drop'. The flood which
ensued brought the food supply. Thus the star was not only
the Great Mother of all, but the sustainer of all.

The brightest stars were regarded as being the greatest
and most influential. In Babylonia all the planets were iden-
tified with great deities. Jupiter, for instance, was Merodach,
and one of the astral forms of Ishtar was Venus. Merodach
was also connected with 'the fish of Ea' (Pisces), so that it
is not improbable that Ea worship had stellar associations.
Constellations were given recognition before the planets were
identified.

*

A god might assume various forms; he might take the form
of an insect, like Indra, and hide in a plant, or become a
mouse, or a serpent, like the gods of Erech in the Gilgamesh
epic. In Egypt, Osiris was the moon, which came as a beau-
tiful child each month and was devoured as the wasting 'old
moon' by the demon Set; he was the young god who was

slain in his prime each year; he was at once the father, husband, and son of Isis; he was the Patriarch who reigned over men and became the Judge of the Dead; he was the earth spirit, he was the bisexual Nile spirit, he was the spring sun; he was the Apis bull of Memphis, and the ram of Mendes; he was the reigning Pharaoh. In his fusion with Ra, who was threefold—Khepera, Ra, and Tum—he died each day as an old man; he appeared in heaven at night as the constellation Orion, which was his ghost, or was, perhaps, rather the Sumerian Zi, the spiritual essence of life. Osiris, who resembled Tammuz, a god of many forms also, was addressed as follows in one of the Isis chants:

> There proceedeth from thee the strong Orion in heaven at
>   evening, at the resting of every day!
> Lo it is I (Isis), at the approach of the Sothis (Sirius) period,
>   who doth watch for him (the child Osiris),
> Nor will I leave off watching for him; for that which
>   proceedeth from thee (the living Osiris) is revered.
> An emanation from thee causeth life to gods and men,
>   reptiles and animals, and they live by means thereof.
> Come thou to us from thy chamber, in the day when thy soul
>   begetteth emanations,—
> The day when offerings upon offerings are made to thy spirit,
>   which causeth the gods and men likewise to live.[1]

This extract emphasises how unsafe it is to confine certain deities within narrow limits by terming them simply 'solar gods', 'lunar gods', 'astral gods', or 'earth gods'. One deity may have been simultaneously a sun god and moon god, an air god and an earth god, one who was dead and also alive, unborn and also old. The priests of Babylonia and Egypt were less accustomed to concrete and logical definitions than their critics and expositors of the twentieth century.

Simple explanations of ancient beliefs are often by reason
of their very simplicity highly improbable. Recognition
must ever be given to the puzzling complexity of religious
thought in Babylonia and Egypt, and to the possibility that
even to the priests, the doctrines of a particular cult, which
embraced the accumulated ideas of centuries, were invari-
ably confusing and vague, and full of inconsistencies; they
were mystical in the sense that the understanding could not
grasp them, although it permitted their acceptance. A god,
for instance, might be addressed at once in the singular and
plural, perhaps because he had developed from an animistic
group of spirits, or, perhaps, for reasons we cannot discover.
This is shown clearly by the following pregnant extract from
a Babylonian tablet: 'Powerful, O Sevenfold, one are ye'.
Mr. L.W. King, the translator, comments upon it as follows:
'There is no doubt that the name was applied to a group of
gods who were so closely connected that, though addressed
in the plural, they could in the same sentence be regarded as
forming a single personality'.[2]

Like the Egyptian Osiris, the Babylonian Merodach was a
highly complex deity. He was the son of Ea, god of the deep;
he died to give origin to human life when he commanded
that his head should be cut off so that the first human beings
might be fashioned by mixing his blood with the earth; he
was the wind god, who gave 'the air of life'; he was the deity of
thunder and the sky; he was the sun of spring in his Tammuz
character; he was the daily sun, and the planets Jupiter and
Mercury as well as Sharru (Regulus); he had various astral
associations at various seasons. Ishtar, the goddess, was Iku
(Capella), the water channel star, in January-February, and
Merodach was Iku in May-June. This strange system of iden-
tifying the chief deity with different stars at different peri-
ods, or simultaneously, must not be confused with the mon-
otheistic identification of him with other gods. Merodach

changed his forms with Ishtar, and had similarly many forms.
This goddess, for instance, was, even when connected with
one particular heavenly body, liable to change. According to
a tablet fragment she was, as the planet Venus, 'a female at
sunset and a male at sunrise'[3] —that is, a bisexual deity like
Nannar of Ur, the father and mother deity combined, and Isis
of Egypt. Nannar is addressed in a famous hymn:

> Father Nannar, Lord, God Sin, ruler among the gods...
> *Mother body which produceth all things...*
> Merciful, gracious Father, in whose hand the life of the whole
> land is contained.

One of the Isis chants of Egypt sets forth, addressing
Osiris:

> There cometh unto thee Isis, lady of the horizon, who hath
> begotten herself alone in the image of the gods...
> She hath taken vengeance before Horus, *the woman who was
> made a male by her father Osiris.*[4]

Merodach, like Osiris-Sokar, was a 'lord of many
existences', and likewise 'the mysterious one, he who is
unknown to mankind'.[5] It was impossible for the human
mind 'a greater [mind] than itself to know'.

Evidence has not yet been forthcoming to enable us
to determine the period at which the chief Babylonian
deities were identified with the planets, but it is clear
that Merodach's ascendancy in astral form could not have
occurred prior to the rise of that city god of Babylon as
chief of the pantheon by displacing Enlil. At the same time
it must be recognised that long before the Hammurabi age
the star-gazers of the Tigro-Euphrates valley must have been
acquainted with the movements of the chief planets and

stars, and, no doubt, they connected them with seasonal changes as in Egypt, where Isis was identified with Sirius long before the Ptolemaic age, when Babylonian astronomy was imported. Horus was identified not only with the sun but also with Saturn, Jupiter, and Mars.[6]

It is of special interest to find that the stars were grouped by the Babylonians at the earliest period in companies of seven. The importance of this magical number is emphasised by the group of seven demons which rose from the deep to rage over the land. Perhaps the sanctity of Seven was suggested by Orion, the Bears, and the Pleiad, one of which constellations may have been the 'Sevenfold' deity addressed as 'one'. At any rate arbitrary groupings of other stars into companies of seven took place, for references are made to the seven Tikshi, the seven Lumashi, and the seven Mashi, which are older than the signs of the Zodiac; so far as can be ascertained these groups were selected from various constellations. When the five planets were identified, they were associated with the sun and moon and connected with the chief gods of the Hammurabi pantheon. A bilingual list in the British Museum arranges the sevenfold planetary group in the following order:

> The moon, Sin.
> The sun, Shamash.
> Jupiter, Merodach.
> Venus, Ishtar.
> Saturn, Ninip (Nirig).
> Mercury, Nebo.
> Mars, Nergal.

An ancient name of the moon was Aa, Â, or Ai, which recalls the Egyptian Aâh or Ah. The Sumerian moon was Aku, 'the measurer', like Thoth of Egypt, who in his lunar character as a Fate measured out the lives of men, and was a god of architects, mathematicians and scribes. The moon was the parent of the sun or its spouse, and might be male, or female, or both as a bisexual deity.

As the 'bull of light' Jupiter had solar associations; he was also the shepherd of the stars, a title shared by Tammuz as Orion; Nin-Girsu, a developed form of Tammuz, was identified with both Orion and Jupiter.

Ishtar's identification with Venus is of special interest. When that planet was at its brightest phase, its rays were referred to as 'the beard' of the goddess; she was the 'bearded Aphrodite'—a bisexual deity evidently. The astrologers regarded the bright Venus as lucky and the rayless Venus as unlucky.

Saturn was Nirig, who is best known as Ninip, a deity who was displaced by Enlil, the elder Bel, and afterwards regarded as his son. His story has not been recovered, but from the references made to it there is little doubt that it was a version of the widespread myth about the elder deity who was slain by his son, as Saturn was by Jupiter and Dyaus by Indra. It may have resembled the lost Egyptian myth which explained the existence of the two Horuses—Horus the elder, and Horus, the posthumous son of Osiris. At any rate, it is of interest to find in this connection that in Egypt the planet Saturn was Her-Ka, 'Horus the Bull'. Ninip was also identified with the bull. Both deities were also connected with the spring sun, like Tammuz, and were terrible slayers of their enemies. Ninip raged through Babylonia like a storm flood, and Horus swept down the Nile, slaying the followers of Set. As the divine sower of seed, Ninip may have developed from Tammuz as Horus did from Osiris. Each were at once the father and the son, different forms of the same deity at various seasons of the year. The elder god was displaced by the son (spring), and when the son grew old his son slew him in turn. As the planet Saturn, Ninip was the ghost of the elder god, and as the son of Bel he was the solar war god of spring, the great wild bull, the god of fertility. He was also as Ber 'lord of the wild boar', an animal associated with Rimmon.[7]

Nebo (Nabu), who was identified with Mercury, was a god of Borsippa. He was a messenger and 'announcer' of the gods, as the Egyptian Horus in his connection with Jupiter was Her-ap-sheta, 'Horus the opener of that which is secret'.[8] Nebo's original character is obscure. He appears to have been a highly developed deity of a people well advanced in civilisation when he was exalted as the divine patron of Borsippa. Although Hammurabi ignored him, he was sub-sequently invoked with Merodach, and had probably much in common with Merodach. Indeed, Merodach was also identified with the planet Mercury. Like the Greek Hermes, Nebo was a messenger of the gods and an instructor of mankind. Jastrow regards him as 'a counterpart of Ea', and says: 'Like Ea, he is the embodiment and source of wisdom. The art of writing—and therefore of all literature—is more particularly associated with him. A common form of his name designates him as the "god of the stylus"'.[9] He appears also to have been a developed form of Tammuz, who was an incarnation of Ea. Professor Pinches shows that one of his names, Mermer, was also a non-Semitic name of Ramman.[10] Tammuz resembled Ramman in his character as a spring god of war. It would seem that Merodach as Jupiter displaced at Babylon Nebo as Saturn, the elder god, as Bel Enlil displaced the elder Ninip at Nippur.

The god of Mars was Nergal, the patron deity of Cuthah,[11] who descended into the Underworld and forced into submis-sion Eresh-ki-gal (Persephone), with whom he was afterwards associated. His 'name', says Professor Pinches, 'is supposed to mean "lord of the great habitation", which would be a parallel to that of his spouse, Eresh-ki-gal'.[12] At Erech he symbolised the destroying influence of the sun, and was accompanied by the demons of pestilence. Mars was a planet of evil, plague, and death; its animal form was the wolf. In Egypt it was called Herdesher, 'the Red Horus', and in Greece it was associated with Ares (the Roman Mars), the war god, who assumed his boar form to slay Adonis (Tammuz).

Nergal was also a fire god like the Aryo-Indian Agni, who, as has been shown, links with Tammuz as a demon slayer and a god of fertility. It may be that Nergal was a specialised form of Tammuz, who, in a version of the myth, was reputed to have entered the Underworld as a conqueror when claimed by Eresh-ki-gal, and to have become, like Osiris, the lord of the dead. If so, Nergal was at once the slayer and the slain.

The various Babylonian deities who were identified with the planets had their characters sharply defined as members of an organised pantheon. But before this development took place, certain of the prominent heavenly bodies, perhaps all the planets, were evidently regarded as manifestations of one deity, the primeval Tammuz, who was a form of Ea, or of the twin deities Ea and Anu. Tammuz may have been the 'sevenfold one' of the hymns. At a still earlier period the stars were manifestations of the Power whom those who dwelt in the jungles of Chota Nagpur attempted to propitiate—the 'World Soul' of the Brahmans of the post-Vedic Indian Age. As much is suggested by the resemblances which the conventionalised planetary deities bear to Tammuz, whose attributes they symbolised, and by the Egyptian conception that the sun, Jupiter, Saturn, and Mars were manifestations of Horus. Tammuz and Horus may have been personifications of the Power or World Soul.

Adapted for Reliquiae by the Editors

Author's Notes:

1   J.T. Dennis, *The Burden of Isis*, p. 24.

2   L.W. King, *Babylonian Magic and Sorcery*, p. 117.

3   T.G. Pinches, *Babylonian and Assyrian Religion*, p. 100.

4   J.T. Dennis, *The Burden of Isis*, p. 49.

5   Ibid., p. 52.

6   A. Wiedemann, *Religion of the Ancient Egyptians*, p. 30.

7   A.H. Sayce, *Religion of the Ancient Babylonians*, p. 153, n. 6.

8   A. Wiedemann, *Religion of the Ancient Egyptians*, p. 30.

9   Morris Jastrow (Trans.), *Aspects of Religious Belief and Practice in Babylonia and Assyria*, p. 95.

10 T.G. Pinches, *Babylonian and Assyrian Religion*, pp. 63, 83.

11 When the King of Assyria transported the Babylonians, &c., to Samaria 'the men of Cuth made Nergal', *Old Testament*, King James Version, *2 Kings*, xvii, 30.

12 T.G. Pinches, *Babylonian and Assyrian Religion*, p. 80.

Hotòmqam

Orion

wuuwu'yam

totem

Pavayoykyasi

symbol of the rain spirit

muyqatsiptu

to become a new moon

Sarah Berti
Five Poems

Song of the Deermage

wolf i made you a song of antlers
when the moonwood comes for you wolf
i sang you a deer

wolf i dreamed you the whitetail
when the snowmoon burns for you wolf
i witched you a hart

wolf i inside you outside hunger-time
when the mouth secretes for you wolf
i bound you a fawn

wolf i spun cloven and red-stamped the snowfall
i am the doe now come for you wolf
be afraid i am here wolf

i killed you a deer

Until the Omens Have Gone Dark

until you hear the last leaf
has fallen from my tree

and the spore and mycorrhiza
have returned the spine to humus

and the numinous flamesap of
vein and memory
has grown dark—

for give and make and take
for granted that

the sunfire tipping off
the mountain tor

and the thunderheads
mushrooming in silver

and the soul lion stealing
the foothills of poems

and the detonation
of wildflowers
along the song coast

are my binding omens
to you

At Midnight the Coywolves

at midnight
the coywolves take back their tongues
from human libraries

animal again
we know by

      fur-photon, blood, and the spiral
      howl

that we must
hunt   something
for which we have no

      name

lay down your alphabet

at the mindprints of our sacred paws
surrender the salivating jaws
of your word traps

and flee

at the speed

       of   true
              language

The Original Speech

there are no languages
left to sell

and the trees pine
to touch you without word

and the living Leaves
bearing the unknown Images
of your first magic

are the
original pages

scripted by a holy
Wind that Knows

nothing

Translating Gods

love is a Kōan
of ice
and fire

From Navajo Folklore
Naye-e Sin / War-Song

    Pesh ashike ni shli—yi-na,
    Pesh ashike ni shli—ya-e

Nayenezrani shi ni shli—kola
    Pesh ashike ni shli—
          E-na

Pesh tilyilch-iye shi ke—kola,
    Pesh ashike ni shli—
          E-na

Pesh tilyilch-iye siskle—kola,
    Pesh ashike ni shli—
          E-na

Pesh tilyilch-iye shi e—kola,
    Pesh ashike ni shli—
          E-na

Pesh tilyilch-iye shi tsha—kola
    Pesh ashike ni shli—
          E-na

Nolienni tshina shi-ye
Shi yiki holon-e—kola,
    Pesh ashike ni shli—
          E-na

Lo, the flint youth, he am I,
        The flint youth.

Nayenezrani, Lo, behold me, he am I,
Lo, the flint youth, he am I,
        The flint youth.

Moccasins of black flint have I;
Lo, the flint youth, he am I,
        The flint youth.

Leggings of black flint have I;
Lo, the flint youth, he am I,
        The flint youth.

Tunic of black flint have I;
Lo, the flint youth, he am I,
        The flint youth.

Bonnet of black flint have I;
Lo, the flint youth, he am I,
        The flint youth.

Clearest, purest flint the heart
Living strong within me—heart of flint;
Lo, the flint youth, he am I,
        The flint youth.

Ka' itsiniklizhi-ye
Din-ikwo
Sitzan nahatilch—kola,
Din-ikwo
Pesh ashike ni shli—
E-na

Tsini nahatilch ki la
Nihoka hastoyo-la
Whe-e-yoni-sin-iye

Yoya aiyinilch—kola,
Pesh ashike ni shli—
E-na

Ka' sa-a narai,
Ka' binihotsitti shi ni shli—kola,
Pesh ashike ni shli—
E-na

Pesh ashike ni shli—kola
Pesh ashike ni shli—ya-e.

Now the zig-zag lightnings four
From me flash,
Striking and returning,
From me flash;
Lo, the flint youth, he am I,
The flint youth.

There where'er the lightnings strike,
Into the ground they hurl the foe—
Ancient folk with evil charms.

One upon another, dashed to earth;
Lo, the flint youth, he am I,
The flint youth.

Living evermore,
Feared of all forevermore,
Lo, the flint youth, he am I,
The flint youth.

Lo, the flint youth, he am I,
The flint youth.

Constance Naden
Four Poems

The Last Druid

Despairing and alone,
Where mountain winds make moan,
My days are spent:
Each sacred wood and cave
Is a forgotten grave
Where none lament.

This is my native sod,
But to a stranger God
My people pray;
Till to myself I seem
A scarce remembered dream
When morn is gray.

I know not what I seek;
My heart is cold and weak,
My eyes are dim:
Across the vale I hear
An anthem glad and clear,
The Christians' hymn.

Oh, Christ, to whom they sing,
Thou art not yet the King
Of this wild spot;
I am too weary now
At new-made shrines to bow;
I know Thee not.

They say, when death is o'er
Man lives for evermore
In heaven or hell;
They call Thee Love and Light:
Alas! they may be right,
I cannot tell.

But if in truth Thou live,
If to mankind Thou give
Life, motion, breath;
If Love and Light Thou be,
No longer torture me,
But grant me death.

Give me not heaven, but rest;
In earth's all-sheltering breast
Hide me from scorn:
The gods I served are slain;
My life is lived in vain;
Why was I born?

Gone is the ancient race;
Earth has not any place
For such as I:
Nothing is true but grief;
I have outlived belief,
Then let me die.

These dim, deserted skies
To aged heart and eyes
No comfort give:
Woe to my hoary head!
Woe! for the gods are dead,
And yet I live.

Undiscerned Perfection

Beyond the realm of dull and slumberous Night
I long have wandered with unwearied feet;
The land where Poetry and Science meet
Streaks the far distance with a magic light:
Fair visions glide before my dazzled sight,
And shine, and change, and pass with motion fleet,
But never clear, and steadfast, and complete
In one transcendent brilliancy unite.

I know, the seeming discord is but mine;
The glory is too great for mortal eyes,
All powerless to discover the divine
And perfect harmony of earth and skies:
I know that each confused and tortuous line,
To fuller sight, in true perspective lies.

Evening

From the German of Goethe

O'er every mountain height
Slumber broods,
Scarcely a zephyr light
Stirs in the woods
One leafy crest;
The song-bird sleeps on the bough.
Wait a little, and thou,
Thou too, shalt rest.

The Eye

From the German of Emil Rittershaus

The human soul—a world in little;
The world—a greater human soul;
The eye of man—a radiant mirror,
That clear and true reflects the whole.

And, as in every eye thou meetest
The mirrored image is thine own,
Each mortal sees his soul reflected,
In all the world himself alone.

Gaspar Orozco
Alminar / Minaret (Excerpt)

El corazón de la paloma es una amatista, suspendida en el
aire. Arde. Justo arriba de mis ojos. La hora cerca el lugar
desde el que transmito: que daría por el ladrido negro de un
perro a la distancia. Pero ahora el silencio es tiempo y arena
y caminos desiertos y ola inaudible. Círculos concéntricos
hasta el resplandor que llegará pronto de detrás de los
montes, los montes que son puerta del desierto. Mientras
tanto ¿por qué refulge tan intensa la amatista? ¿por qué su
latido deja una fisura en el metal cromado del cráneo? Con
torpeza, trato de alcanzar la llamita morada, pero este fuego
no se deja tocar. *Este fuego no se deja tocar.*

The dove's heart is an amethyst, suspended in midair. It burns. Just above my eyes. The time of day besieges the place from which I relay: what I wouldn't give for the black bark of a dog in the distance. But now silence is time and sand and desert roads and an inaudible wave. Concentric circles ending in a radiance that will emerge from beyond the hills, the hills that are the gateway to the desert. Meanwhile, why does the amethyst throb such intense light? Why does its pulsing split my chrome skull? Clumsily, I reach out for the little purple flame, but this flame won't let itself be touched. *This flame won't let itself be touched.*

Translated from Spanish by Ilana Luna

Elizabeth-Jane Burnett
Two Poems

Lupin Aphid

As frozen dew the coat of you dusts light,
a brief touch, a whisper of wax
on a body just the colour of the sea.

You live your whole life in one flower.
This, the furthest out you've ever been.
Banished, perhaps, by wolves, by leaves,

by howling roots that tire of the ground.
But every time they take you back: the roots,
the wolves, the leaves; as if they know they moonless go
who go without your sheen.

Ghost Moth

salt	wings
marsh	over
shallow	grass
soil	salt
shingle	marsh
marram	silver
grass	path
fescue	of
grass	pollen
tidal	flight
path	of
creek	swollen
of	night
pollen	calls
falls	flings
in whispers	

Tìikuywùuti

the spiritual mother of all hunted animals

wisoko

buzzard

soo'ala

star horn (a constellation)

wa'wa'oo wa'wa'

sound a coyote makes

Michael Goodfellow
Book of Days

Drawing for a dug well—how the well ran salty—how ocean
surged the brook—and the drought-dried ground soaked
it up—how if love was rust—then what the metal it's made
of—what the rain that fell—then how the well filled—how
life was copper pipe and lead flashing—glazier's tips against
cut glass—foot valve sucking the flooded dark—something
rocked in—how a kind of mortar held it together—then how
the taps ran brine—salt a smear of blood on the lips—dew
you said, it dried clear

Cold frame—leaves the bones of themselves—sky the dead
skin of itself—dirt buckled by frost—I pull rocks from the
weighted frame—ironstone dug from the brook—husks
and dried vines clung—to the frayed nylon, a tangle of
plastic—against hollow metal—water pours from the
frame—as it tilts down the basement stairs—anything can
be pulled apart—hauled down to some place—for another
winter, that was one thing—but not half, it was how shallow
the roots go—how loose the hold—how any hand could run
through soil—and lift it up—that any stone had give—like
a bulb, then how your body did

Burnt back—pit filled with soot and char—after a winter of
fires, you dug hard—bent over the stone circle—shovelled
arm after arm—into the wheeled barrel—metal blackened,
ash—foamed, thud—the thump of wet snow—once full,
dump it past—the compost pile—to kill the poison ivy
back—leaves hot metal to cold flesh—a bright spot—where
the skin held tight—it grew, let it burn—you thought—it
burned now let it rot

Hop bar—metal slammed—to leave—a hole—water—the
suck—of wet dirt—old mud—hand against—cold soil—heart
wood—hard roots

Fall mow—last lug of oil—thick blade—through thin
grass—last pour—of clear gas, mouth hardened—by dirt
and grease—cap pulled tight—cord yanked out—how dry
grass—thundered to life—under the low hood—spat against
tempered hull—*flug flug flug*—against chipped flap—yet
still—the blade took hold—flame wants that—stalk to be
cut down—better for ground—to harden, stones—to push
up—through dead frost

A handbook of roses — we wait all spring for the boxed
rose — in a marked glassine — bark damp, half dead — roots
tipped with mold — we picked 'Heathcliff' from the
book — named *A Handbook of Roses* — pulled from a stack
of manilla envelopes — and seed catalogues and dug its
hole — by the dry stream bed, wide — to let spring roots
spread — through manure mixed with river mud — and
rockweed, leaves and peat — *a bushy habit, the scent of*
tea — you read out loud — it needed lots — liquid dead
fish — and powdery blocks — of dried moss — later winter
hung — like a kind of rough cloth — blooms curled,
leaves — the colour of rock

Checking the well after rain — the path of salvaged bricks to
the brook — a well crock turned to make a bridge — then scrub
on the other side — alder, mayflower, birch — and the well's
cracked skirt — suck of air to lift the stone plug — humid with
a summer's warmth — then sow bugs on the well stones and
water, foot valve stuck like a broken leg — against flooded
ground — you could call it what it meant to live — saunter,
beauty, then a hard pull — and the built pit

Erin Wilson
Three Poems

Corm of Cyclamen

Silent room
Earthen hollow
Hallowed be thy frame

Unveiled vial
Virtuous veil
Blessed walls of possibility

You, my, me, amaranthine finitude
Thee, quake, seeking source and solitude

Blessed be the crack, the fissure
Blessed be the stock-still, maintaining air's form for the
        moment
Blessed be the vacuum, which lends residence to the
        gleaming seed

Have harangued the chains holding this empty vessel
Have bemoaned the meagerness of naught and space
Have bejewelled the self in splendid stars of sorrow

Yet, corm of cyclamen
Storage house of ether
Brief chance,
            dearest

Exigent, This: That

Words such as *desire* or *need* or —
    requirement

The body born of the bowl
The bowl born of the node which was born of the body

Always the mind seeking the word
Always the word seeking the body

I could say, *I go to the woods to return home*
but I'd have to add, *I'm coming, but I'll not arrive*

Jack pine, red pine, pitch pine, hackmatack
A knife in the hand, a blind blade hacking

Always the *via negativa*
Always the shadows of the firs

In the Presence Of

Wanting to know the real world,
the world beyond the soot of self,

I decanted that night with the wolf
and set it on the bookshelf,

pressed it like a flower between the words fæger and hwīt,
hlūtor and clæne,

left it there for years, quietly,
while I walked off into forests

and itched while watching owls
and scratched while watching stars,

until my skin scuffed off
and fell like eiderdown down,

and was again like milkweed's last spike
to its ragged refuge,

until it too was gone even in its likeness,

and I was finally pure enough to understand the eyes that
    held neither
right nor wrong, or resulting drama,

not one iota of conspicuous conscience,
or lack of scruple,

no name like victim,
no name like foe,

only eyes mathematically mitigating withdrawal or approach,
freosan infinitude.

Kabir
Five Poems

IV

        I. 58. bāgo nā jā re nā jā

Do not go to the garden of flowers!
O Friend! go not there;
In your body is the garden of flowers.
Take your seat on the thousand petals
    of the lotus, and there gaze on the
    Infinite Beauty.

VII

I. 85. sādho, Brahm alakh lakhāyā

When He Himself reveals Himself,
  Brahma brings into manifestation
  That which can never be seen.
As the seed is in the plant, as the shade
  is in the tree, as the void is in the
  sky, as infinite forms are in the
  void—
So from beyond the Infinite, the
  Infinite comes; and from the In-
  finite the finite extends.
The creature is in Brahma, and
  Brahma is in the creature: they
  are ever distinct, yet ever united.
He Himself is the tree, the seed, and
  the germ.
He Himself is the flower, the fruit,
  and the shade.
He Himself is the sun, the light, and
  the lighted.
He Himself is Brahma, creature, and
  Maya.
He Himself is the manifold form, the
  infinite space;
He is the breath, the word, and the
  meaning.

He Himself is the limit and the limit-
    less: and beyond both the limited
    and the limitless is He, the Pure
    Being.
He is the Immanent Mind in Brahma
    and in the creature.

The Supreme Soul is seen within the
    soul,
The Point is seen within the Supreme
    Soul,
And within the Point, the reflection
    is seen again.
Kabir is blest because he has this
    supreme vision!

VIII

I. 101 is ghaṭ antar bāg bagīce

Within this earthen vessel are bowers
    and groves, and within it is the
    Creator:
Within this vessel are the seven oceans
    and the unnumbered stars.
The touchstone and the jewel-
    appraiser are within;
And within this vessel the Eternal
    soundeth, and the spring wells
    up.
Kabir says: 'Listen to me, my
    friend! My beloved Lord is with-
    in.'

XII

II. 24. haṃsā, kaho purātan bāt

Tell me, O Swan, your ancient tale.
From what land do you come, O
    Swan? to what shore will you
    fly?
Where would you take your rest, O
    Swan, and what do you seek?

Even this morning, O Swan, awake,
    arise, follow me!
There is a land where no doubt nor
    sorrow have rule: where the terror
    of Death is no more.
There the woods of spring are a-bloom,
    and the fragrant scent 'He is I'
    is borne on the wind:
There the bee of the heart is deeply
    immersed, and desires no other
    joy.

XIV

II. 56. dariyā kī lahar dariyāo hai jī

The river and its waves are one surf:
    where is the difference between the
    river and its waves?
When the wave rises, it is the water;
    and when it falls, it is the same
    water again. Tell me, Sir, where
    is the distinction?
Because it has been named as wave,
    shall it no longer be considered as
    water?

Within the Supreme Brahma, the
    worlds are being told like beads:
Look upon that rosary with the eyes
    of wisdom.

Translated from Hindi by Rabindranath Tagore and Evelyn Underhill

Arvind Krishna Mehrotra
Lockdown Garden (Excerpt)

Watered,
the bloodleaves lose
their droop and glow
in the western sun

under the litchi,
that in April
is covered in blossom,
in May with parrots.

*

Three new basil plants
have sprung up this monsoon,
each three feet apart,

as though the wind
had measured the distance
before dispersing the seeds.

*

Planted as groundcover,
the arrowhead vine mass produces
arrowhead leaves in season
and out, whether you notice or not.

Thus a civilian garden
gets militarised, not that the military
lacks gardens to grow,
in wartime and peace, prize dahlias.

*

I heard a sound,
saw something fall.
What I saw was not
the sound I heard.

The sound I heard
was a mango falling.
What I saw
was a falling leaf.

*

A danger to the house
and too big to cut down,
the silk oak when it falls
will be a ship sinking.

*

When a branch
of the dillenia fell

it was as if a corrugated sheet
had been ripped off the tree.

Behind it, above the garden shed,
rose a blue hill in the distance.

*

I pulled up a stool
and spent a few minutes
beside the Rangoon creeper.

It had been cut back
and was now growing again
through the balusters.

There was a light wind blowing.
After a long time
I heard the caw of a crow.

Let no one tell you
that leaves don't breathe
or cannot listen.

*

Richard Skinner
Two Poems

Caedmon's Hymn

Walking is nothing but a controlled way of falling
pushing forward into still unsecured galleries
and when you enter the dream light chamber
making sure to clamp, not twist, the handles
notice the ammonites frozen in the wall
the sea birds dropping and dipping their wings
as you drop to your knees at the foot of the statue
you are dazzled by the blue star in her belly
the cup of jewels in the hinge of her hands
her blood red eyes are a sharpening stone
as your knees of glass start to score the flags
you realise there is still a passageway forward
and this alabaster frieze of grief
shows you grief is nothing but a release of love

A Patch of Birch

A square
layout of
silver needles,
spindles of
glowing leaves.

In the grid
the birdsong
is shrill, they sing
This is not
the real world.

Alton Melvar M. Dapanas
Self-Portrait as Wak-wak

I come as a midnight birdsong, a skyward incantation
of evil. With clawed wings that resemble risk, my forelimbs
seek heat of your flesh, warmth of your soul.

And as I rouse you from your even breathing, I face in
you what I could say is part-anger, part-fear, all the unnam-
able feelings in between. But nothing can split the quiet:
crows and owls migrate to the farthest trees, the cicadas in
the nearest bush turn muted, the fireflies settle lightless in
the dead street lamp, even the wind stops. They sense death.

Between the two of us, young sad boy, not a single word,
only your screams, gibberish plea for help, and my drawl.

Do not be mistaken that I will spare you or that you can
remake me in your image, appealing to the human in me
as you hasten a thousand signs of the cross bereft of belief.
What I can wordlessly promise is this: I will list your name
in my head, memorise each dark spot and bone before I take
them in.

So as I devour you, I cram your miserable life, I glut on your entirety. You will be in me, in the clandestine spaces of my insides, like the others long consumed before you.

Before the hint of dawn, I go back in hiding after painting this bloody makeshift town. This is a routine of coming full out of the dark. Because such is the bestial curse of hunger: I cannot stop eating what I love.

But for now, in the literal dead of the night, thin of anything that can bear witness, I suck you dry, I swallow you in.

Author's Note:

In Philippine mythology, the wak-wak is a nocturnal shape-shifting monster, believed to hunt humans and other animals for food.

tamavutskoho

jawbone

kiskya

passageway

qööyi

scorched on the body

homvȍöta

to consecrate a pathway for spirit beings

Gustav Meyrink
Fakir Paths

Introduction by Frater Acher

Nihil Scire—Omnia Posse.
—*Gustav Meyrink*

Meyrink's 'novels' thus are literature only in a very conditional sense, they
are rather in their lucent mask, not unlike Apuleius' 'Metamorphoses' or
Joséphin Péladan's 'novels', in truth an esoteric apocalypse.[1]
—*Henri Birven*

Gustav Meyrink's short essay 'Fakir Paths' ('Fakirpfade') was
first published in the August issue of *März—Halbmonatsschrift*
für deutsche Kultur, 1907, which at the beginning of the
twentieth century was one of the most successful bi-monthly
journals in Germany.

In April of the same year, Meyrink had previously pub-
lished an essay entitled 'Fakire'; thus 'Fakirpfade' was writ-
ten as a direct follow-up to the discussion of a subject that
was hugely popular at this time, that of alleged Indian fakirs
who toured his homeland in circuses, demonstrating their
apparently occult capabilities.

What follows is a new English translation of this second
essay. Due to Meyrink's extravagant use of punctuation, the
text has been slightly adjusted to provide a uninterrupted
reading experience. This short introduction intends to shine
a preliminary light on the many layers of advanced occult
knowledge contained in this short text.

Meyrink's literary legacy mainly consists of his famed
occult novels, as well as several collections of short stories.
The moments when we hear the author speak directly to us,
unmediated by symbolic characters, are very rare. Meyrink
left us with less than a dozen essays in which he provides
direct expertise and instructions on how to navigate esoteric
worlds. This preference to speak to the reader, not in his own
voice, but through a carefully curated ensemble of mythi-
cal beings, archetypical personas, occult events, visionary
dreams and distant memories, is a critical characteristic of
Meyrink's oeuvre and holds an essential key to understand-
ing his approach to the magical realm. Despite the fact that
Meyrink was an active member of several occult lodges and
orders, both in the Eastern and Western Hemisphere, his
own creative output is essentially anti-traditionalist and
rather existentialist.

> When I was still a young person and digging up with ardour
> everything that looked halfway like the secrets of magic and
> yoga, I entered into such brotherhoods by the dozens and
> had to take oaths that would have caused the skin to shudder,
> oaths of secrecy about things that at that time had already
> become common knowledge to myself and beyond myself. In
> the end, I simply refused to be initiated further into these
> 'terrible' secrets, due to the unpleasant feeling that in the end
> I would even have to keep secret that two times two is four.[2]

By the time he wrote 'Fakirpfade', Meyrink had not yet
published any of his famous novels. And yet he had already
undergone more than fifteen years of a self-inflicted, grim
and ardent regime of daily yoga- and occult-exercises. He
had become friends with the famous practical alchemist
Alexander Bernus (1880–1965), himself a keen student of
inner and outer alchemy. He had joined the Golden Dawn,

as well as the Theosophical Society, where he received direct instruction from Annie Besant (1847–1933). He had acquired advanced knowledge in theoretical and applied Kabbalah, had dedicated himself to the practical mystical teachings of J.B. Kerning (1774–1851) and Alois Mailänder (1843–1905), had rediscovered the works of P.B. Randolph (1825–1875) and went on to publish them, and, of course, he was in ongoing correspondence with several authentic Indian yogis, who promised to initiate him into their paths.

Against this background, we encounter the author of 'Fakirpfade', still six years away from the release of his breakthrough novel *Der Golem*, and yet already on the steep ascent to becoming one of the most accomplished and reclusive occult adepts of his time. Most of all, Meyrink was a man who spoke from *lived* mystical and magical experience, from an earned place of proximity to the Divine, and who maintained an iron resolution not to become entangled in the occult revival of 'ancient' orders, nor in the magical appropriation of Eastern or Egyptian initiatory traditions, which was occurring all around him in the early twentieth century.

Meyrink preferred the artistic form of the novel or novella to technical occult primers and guidebooks precisely because of this *lived* occult experience. He was able to clearly see the dangers and pitfalls that codified answers present for any mystical path. Therefore, instead of pressing his own experience into cut and dry forms and attempting to mass-produce occult results, he went on a lifelong literary journey attempting to hand over the actual mystical spark to his readers, free from human-made traditions. Meyrink's highest goal was one of genuine *spiritual simultaneity*. Being equally grounded in the world of natural creation and the higher realms, expanding one's consciousness to see clearly both in the mundane and in the visionary realms at once, and becoming the actual bridge that spans between this life and the afterlife, not as metaphor, but as mystical first-hand experience derived from decades of ardent practice. This is the reason Meyrink abhorred all traditional symbolism, why he preferred the language of dreams and visions over the pseudo-accuracy of occult terminology, and why he often wrote with vitriolic sharpness about the magical revival taking place around him.

Meyrink's approach to occult teaching was intention-ally riverine; unapologetically ambiguous, always flowing around key words, sparing technical references, and entirely focussed upon enabling the reader to receive a glimpse of what it means to stand in true proximity to the living magic beyond the threshold of numb, everyday interactions. Meyrink was obsessed with inducing *magical awakeness.*

In an unpublished manuscript, we find Meyrink writing of himself in the third person, giving us a self-description of 'the author'. He is unmistakably clear that he does not understand his work as literature or art, but as practically applied magic:

> Position on literature and poetry: none. He states that his own works have nothing to do with it. [...]

> He says: What he writes is 'magic' — suggestion — and is not bound to the rules and recipes of 'art composition' or the like — thus it has only very few points of contact with what the chief teachers of all subjects understand by 'art' and literature. He also does not believe that it is possible to pass a uniform judgement on his works, precisely because they are magic — suggestion — and they must awaken in each individual reader different images, thoughts, ideas and feelings. This is their precise purpose, and the endeavour to do justice to 'rules of art' is far from them.[3]

In light of this, Meyrink's essay 'Fakirpfade' is much
more than a casual commentary by a Western adept on the
common misunderstandings which occur upon the path of
yoga.

Woven through allusions and apparently incidental
references, we encounter several of the essential themes
that would later on comprise the fabric of his magical
novels: the ambiguous identification of the true guru as
an 'Anderer' (*other one*) is a hint toward the phantom-like
gestalt omnipresent in all of Meyrink's key works, and which
is referred to in loose terms as the 'Lotse' (*pilot* or *guide*) or
the 'Vermummte' (*hooded* or *masked one*). The explanation
of unconscious trance as a negative side effect to be avoided,
points towards Meyrink's life-long purpose of 'becoming a
bridge of life' which spans between the inner and the outer
realms.[4]

The centre of the current essay, however, is dedicated
to Meyrink's eruditions on the strange effects that take
place once the student has successfully liberated from their
physical body what the author calls the 'gestaltlose Kraft'
(*formless force*). Once freed, this spirit-like force is able to
roam amongst the countless shells attached to the soul of the
student, which the formless force then randomly animates
until these shells have been 'burned off'; only then can the
formless force travel with genuine purpose and without
distraction. Meyrink's precise description of this complex
process avoids entanglement in orthodox terms, and instead
explains a most sophisticated spiritual process in plain,
everyday language, free of references from any particular
spiritual tradition.

Nevertheless, the intimate student of Meyrink's work
sees the indirect reference to the Vedanta teachings, with
which the author was deeply familiar, both in theory and
practice. In fact, in one of his more cynical early novellas

(*Der Herr Kommerzienrat Kuno Hinrichsen und der Büßer Lalaladschpat-Rai*, in *Fledermäuse*, 1917) we find the same notion condensed into the final ironic outcry of the protagonist: '"Tat twam asi"—the whole gang is me after all.' Equally, in his magnum opus on the magical life of the Renaissance magician John Dee (*Der Engel vom Westlichen Fenster*, 1927) we encounter almost an entire novel dedicated to the idea of freeing oneself from the iron grip of these 'accompanying beings' who dwell inside our blood memory, and who can force us into swirling vicious circles of repetition throughout many centuries and incarnations.

Finally, the combination of a mystical state of 'Scheintod' (*apparent death*) with the emergence of a subtle-bodied 'double that can no longer decompose', marks a central theme in Meyrink's oeuvre. Stripped of its traditional integration into Tantric *yidam* practice (David-Néel, pp. 256–260), Jewish kabbalistic *demuth* adoration (Scholem, pp. 249–274) or Neoplatonic conjuration of one's personal *holy daïmon*, Meyrink, in the most succinct manner, takes the reader directly into the physical experience and consequences of such occult phenomena.

Over the decades to follow, Meyrink would explore this theme multiple times. We find it embodied in various guises and presented in the mystical light of his novels, from *Der Golem* to *Das Grüne Gesicht*, to his most occult work, *Der Weiße Dominikaner*.

Meyrink, thus, masterfully transcends the boundaries of any given tradition. In the short essay below he moves through Tibetan, Hindu, Christian and Theosophical references, only to reveal the underlying existential reality of the genuine mystical experience. It was Meyrink's keen concern to make the reader of his works *experience* rather than *understand*. He wrote from the mystic's vantage point, from a place where it becomes evident that nature transcends all human-made traditions, and where one learns that on the search for one's path, it is best to begin with what is one's own — with the experiences and culture one has proximity to — rather than indulging in seemingly exotic or occult cultural contexts.

As 'Fakirpfade' illustrates beautifully, Meyrink's continuous border crossing of human-made traditions is a most deliberate literary device. And this is also how his unusual linguistic style has to be understood: the author's voice continuously dances upon a knife's edge between several reality models. The reader is never certain whether the neologisms of *formless force, other one, accompanying beings,* etc., speak of animistic spirit beings, subtle energy patterns, or psychological reference terms. Meyrink always denied access to easy frames of reference, but instead, induced through the evocative tone of his voice and dream-like stories, he leads the reader out into the open field of their own occult experiences.

In stark contrast to his pompous magical contemporary, Aleister Crowley, Meyrink's approach to teaching magic transcended codified knowledge, and always avoided the straight line. Instead, his novels are an adept's attempt to *speak from heart to heart*, to induce visions within his readers of an inner landscape so that they may stride out independently, and finally begin to sense a delicate light, a most tender voice — that of their own inner selves.

In a letter from 1917 Meyrink expressed the nature of this path in an unusually direct manner:

> I know very well what it means: to so cry out for light, that one is almost scorched in the process — I have cried out all my life, until I was finally found. That's why I can empathise with you and hope to be able to help you soon.

The only thing worth finding is the innermost 'I'; that I
which we are, and always were, without having known it. This
I is always subject, it is pure spirit, free of form, time and
space, with which it has only alloyed itself momentarily. You
are it, but only potentially, not yet consciously. [...]

The innermost I is as delicate as a butterfly—it is the most
subtle, delicate and most natural way one has to go into
the innermost. 'To take by force the kingdom of heaven' is
unsuitable today—and is only for fakirs.[5]

Every era has its 'ways'. The purest way to the innermost is
delicate. Or do you believe that the divine I is deaf, that one
has to shout at it for hours like J.B. Kerning?

The best key is called: joy! Joyful confidence: 'I know that
You, my 'I', are omnipotent even when I do not find You; I
know that nothing I do is sin in Your eyes; may You work the
magic word in me.' Something like this. [6]

Frater Acher, 2021

Fakir Paths

'Blessed art thou with a counsellor at thy bedside.'

The alchemists of the Middle Ages racked their brains for
the means to extract the tincture of eternal life from the dull
lead of earthly existence. The people of today are long past
such a thing—they seek instead to turn the gold of immortal-
ity into greasy banknotes.
     In the windows of bookstores and in the advertisements
of daily papers, instructions abound as to how one can

become an accomplished criminal in five minutes for only one mark—through occult means.

How long until the gentlemen salesmen of life-insurance will study the holy writings of the Vedanta in order to better fox their worthy clientele by virtue of magical breathing exercises?

*

It is true that in our times the stars are favourable for Jill and Joe; domesticated cabbage and herb are tenderly watered, while the noble wild wormwood dies of thirst. A cubic kilometre of rotten manna in the form of theosophical literature has fallen from heaven—and everything is included in these 'mystical' modern books: where the vanished continents of Lemuria and Atlantis are located, how many principles of the soul humans comprise, and also the glad tidings that in Germany, finally, under the spiritual protection of toast-blonde adepts, a completely independent, reformed patriotic-theosophical order has been formed. However, nobody provides the truth about the first steps on the real path, which, as it is said in the fairy tale of the princess Sheherazade, shall lead to the talking bird, to the singing tree, and to the source of resurrection.[1]

More truth can be found in every folk tale than can be found in these 'wisdom writings', but people believe that they have to dig deeply for water in such tales, and therefore do not see the secret of the glittering dew that lies on top.

It is true that the ancient Indian doctrines of yoga, with cold, dry words, appear to offer information about the methods used to acquire the miraculous powers of the fakirs—but just try to follow them!

Plenty of ascetic exercises: Live in solitude. Eat only five bites a day. Assume certain postures that only a contortionist can maintain. Hold your breath, first for five minutes, then ten, twenty, thirty, and so on, up to two hours, and when you have learned all this—and moreover, concentrated your thoughts on the magic words *Bhur* and *Hamsa* until every cell of your body cries out—only then, after yet more special exercises, can you attain mastery over the *siddhis* (miraculous powers).

These precepts will remain completely obscure to anyone unless they know—and our theosophical and mystical master teachers do not know—that all these bodily processes (mudras, asanas etc.), are *effects* and not *causes*, and that they must be preceded by a very definite state during which these breathing adjustments, cardiac effects, etc., occur all by themselves, through a kind of *suspended animation*.

Is it possible to bring about this state, which leads to the gate of yoga, by oneself—for example, by concentrating the thoughts upon a single point? In the teachings it is expressly stated that a guru or 'guide' is indispensable, and in these words lie the key to understanding.

Since this oft-misunderstood sentence has infiltrated our public, our community has been inundated with gurus, secret doctrines and 'guides', intentional and unintentional deceivers. Every other moment, from inside or outside the theosophical, talmi-rosicrucian and other occult brotherhoods, a new trickster appears and pretends to be an initiate who can read the 'astral realm' and provide exercises for the awakening of magical abilities.

The authentic guru cannot be an ordinary person, who eats, drinks and digests, and who has a profession, but should instead be understood as an *other one* (*Anderer*), and even the Indian writings are often confusing rather than open-hearted on this point.

Also, advice or instruction, even from a genuine guru, would be completely useless and inadequate, because the process depends upon the disciple being placed into the aforementioned state of suspended animation directly by the 'guide'. This happens in a way known to, and possible only by, the accomplished yogi acting as a conduit for the guru's will. It is not dissimilar to the Ancient Greek 'psychagogues'. The guru transfers the initiate into this state as often, and for as long, as is required for the disciple to learn how to evoke it by themselves.

Gradually, the duration of the suspended animation becomes shorter and shorter (up to a fraction of a second), until, for the observer, the process is no longer perceived at all. Then the outwardly visible asanas and mudras and other yoga 'exercises' also fall away.

A variation of this suspended animation, the so-called *trance*, occurs with the (few genuine) spiritualistic mediums. These, too, each possess a 'guide'—a controlling spirit, as it is called in technical language—but their 'trance' is not based upon yoga, and only resembles it, such as insanity can resemble genius. Their trance is not the result of careful education, but rather of an innate, purely physical disposition.

Another difference is that the medium falls into deep unconsciousness, and the trance itself is required to make the psychic phenomena possible, whereas the yoga student must experience the suspended animation with its accompanying symptoms (the above mentioned inhibitions of breathing, etc.) at the beginning only, and only until the powers, and the ability to handle them, have been firmly transferred to them by the guru. However, even during the initial stages of authentic yoga, consciousness is never lost. To the contrary—if unconscious trance occurs in a fakir or a dervish, it is always the characteristic of mediumism, and as such is a sign that the psychic faculties are not yet of a permanent nature, and moreover, are linked to a series of preconditions which are not present in the yogi.

The technique of this art, according to its authentic teaching, is to be thought of as follows: by the 'apparent death', as by the trance, the human being is, as it were, divided into two parts—into a purely physical organism, as well as a *formless force* (*gestaltlose Kraft*).

The ordinary human being is perpetually surrounded or afflicted by a chain of (invisible) beings. Over the course of their lifetime, some of these beings die off, some are newly born. Mistakenly, they are often considered the 'souls of the deceased'. If now this *formless force*, or a part of it, becomes liberated in some way, then these beings become strangely animated, and become independent—in a similar, though far more complicated way, as the well-known dead frog of Luigi Galvani under the influence of electricity. The consequences are 'spiritualistic manifestations' in their full strangeness, which seemingly overturn the laws of nature.

With the yoga student, however, the matter is different. In their psyche there are no longer such 'beings'. Through a long process of mortification they have perished, as the thousand heads of the Hydra were destroyed by Hercules. They now surround their master as lifeless bodies and mysterious instruments awaiting his use, circling around him as the burnt-out moon circles the living earth.

The power released in the apparent death of the yogi does not remain formless (as with the medium), but instead gradually coagulates into a shape—the eternally indestructible carrier of the ever-waking consciousness of the yogi beyond sleep, swoon and death—into a double that can no longer decompose.

The nature of this power, which is able to dissolve everything in itself—the 'philosophical Mercury' of the hermetic alchemists—and the effects and laws which it creates and by which it is inhibited, cannot be discussed here. Suffice it to say that by means of it, the most trivial, as well as the most sublime thoughts, i.e. consciously formed intentions, can be equipped and clothed with those external qualities which we call tangibility, visibility, etc., and about whose 'reality' or 'illusion' our modern science has already come to irrefutably precise conclusions.[2]

Only once these 'accompanying beings' have died off in one's psyche can the human being practice yoga or more correctly, *experience* it. And only at that time does the 'guru' come to them—whether at the North Pole, in the Himalayas, in prison, or, as with Saint-Hubert, during the deer hunt.

The process of immolating the 'accompanying beings' can take thousands of years (according to the teachings, the psyche embodies itself again and again) and must not be confused with 'yoga'. For those within whom it has begun—those whom the Uraeus snake of paradise has once bitten—their path turns sharply away from those of their peers. And though they may appear to be among others, in truth they are much, much further away from them than spatial distances are able to separate.

Humans of all nations and centuries bear the wound from the bite of this serpent, and from these multitudes—which have become incalculable in the course of time—an army, tortured by a thirst for the metaphysical, and which rolls itself towards dark goals, has grown—an incomprehensible enigma to others.

'Degenerate', Max Nordau calls those who have been bitten by this serpent; Jesus Christ calls them the salt of the earth.[3]

In the one, the poison of the serpent shows its effect as a dark, incomprehensible drive towards self-torment and asceticism; in the other, as a longing for supernatural power, knowledge and metaphysical insight, or as a religious thirst for the Godhead.

'As the deer pants for streams of water, so my soul pants for you, O God.' (Psalm 42: 1) the Bible says.

If one was to isolate a few from the multitudes of those 'pilgrims', as I will call them—whether they live naked and lonely in forests like Indian Sannyasins or cultivated, as European mystics, among the people—and if one further researched their thoughts and aspirations, the goal of their path and what is the shining light at their feet, one would encounter infinite contradictions.

The miraculous powers that one soul strives for appear to the other as poisonous berries along the way; the delights and raptures of one, appear to the other as vice. Swedenborg shakes his head at Gautama Buddha's delusion and longs for heaven, while the Chinese ascetic Hu-Tzu prolongs his physical life by a thousand years.

And whoever does not succeed in peering more deeply into the chaos will believe they are standing before a chapter in the history of human foolishness.

*

The view only clears when one understands that every 'pilgrim' goes towards the goal of *their longing*, and that the mystical 'way' to the gate of yoga—the burning out of the hydra heads—consists of nothing but the sacrifices one can offer *to* this longing.

The public rarely hears of those who strive towards the royal path, the path of power and omniscience, which the Chinese Hu-Tzu and Chuang-Tzu may have walked; instead they hear of those who long for the bliss of the 'everlasting contemplation of God' and inner enlightenment, those who consider the (miraculous powers of the) Siddhis and everything that is related to the outer world as barriers to their progress.

Jakob Böhme (1575–1624), Jane Leade (1624–1704) and Jeanne-Marie Bouvier de la Motte Guyon (1648–1717) are some of the best known among Europeans, and among Indians, Swami Bhaskarananda Saraswati (1833–1899) from the sect of the Sannyasins, and especially Sri Ramakrishna Paramahamsa (1836–1886).

A few words here about their lives:

Bhaskarananda, born in 1833 into a noble Brahmin family, studied Sanskrit and the philosophy of the Vedas with ardent zeal from the age of eight. When a son was born to him in his eighteenth year, he considered his relations with human beings fulfilled according to the laws of Manu, and in order to 'put into practice' (that is, to practically carry out the secret process of killing off the particular 'attendant beings') his belief in the illusion of the external world, which he had hitherto felt only theoretically, he became a wandering ascetic. More and more he deepened his studies of Vedanta, and in order to reach the ability of inner seeing, he joined the sect of the Sannyasins.

Gradually he experienced those shifts of consciousness and polar changes of the body which form the basis for the practical (not only theoretical) realisation 'that the external world is nothing real, never existed in reality, does not exist, nor will ever exist'. 'Just as we dream in sleep, think what we have dreamed is real, upon awakening must realise beyond all doubt that we have been mistaken, so we can attain another kind of awakening in which the outer world, too, with all its mutual relations and relative laws, is seen through and recognised as insubstantial, as a shadow and a dream-image.'[4]

After thirteen years of asceticism, Bhaskarananda attained the realisation he longed for and remained near

Benares for the rest of his life. He was the object of supreme
reverence to the Hindus, and even Europeans who sought
him out were filled with admiration for the enormous depth
of his knowledge. Miracles of all kinds, especially healings,
are attributed to him.

Sri Ramakrishna Paramahamsa's life story—shared by
the Oxford professor Max Müller[5]—is the most touching,
strange, and at the same time most instructive document in
this field which can be found.

Also born in 1833, Ramakrishna was possessed from
childhood by an incessant, desperate thirst to behold and
unite with the Godhead (whom he fondly visualised as the
Indian goddess Kali). A whole series of miraculous states
beset Ramakrishna, and none of the European physicians
and scholars, who came to Ramakrishna in large numbers as
if drawn to a medical curiosity, understood how to interpret
them. Often he lapsed into suspended animation for days,
and always some naked, silent Sannyasin, as if sent by a
secret power, came along, performed strange manipulations
upon him, and thus brought him back to life. Later, he was
afflicted with an inability to sleep or close his eyes for twelve
full years, as well as other such grievances. All from the des-
perate longing to find God.

A glaring light is thrown upon these kinds of physical
symptoms by the fact that these same processes, in the same
intensity and sequence, according to the holy books of the
'Vaishnava' sect (i.e. devotees of the Hindu god Vishnu) had
been experienced once before—four hundred years previ-
ously—by the religious reformer of Bengal, Sri Chaitanya
Mahaprabhu (1486–1534). Thus they are typical.

Gradually, Ramakrishna's stormy symptoms of dying
abated and gave way to a feeling of indescribable bliss and
delight, which, according to his description, never left him
for even an hour during the rest of his life. And in the same

measure, without having pursued any studies, such a pro-
found wisdom and all-encompassing philosophical knowledge
grew within him, as if out of nowhere, that soon a circle of
Indian (as well as European and American) scholars gathered
around him and listened, with awe, to his teachings.

Sometimes such a strong 'magnetic' radiation emanated
from him that many of his visitors fell into unconsciousness
and catalepsy.

How little he valued 'miraculous powers' is evident from
a remark he made when told about a yogi staying nearby who
had overcome gravity and who at times walked on water. He
merely shook his head pityingly and said, 'How far behind in
true knowledge must this merciful one be!'

Rightly, Ramakrishna can be regarded as the most impor-
tant Indian prophet of recent centuries, and he is the only
one in world history who experienced not only the practical
mysteries of his own religion, but also those of others, such
as Islam and Christianity (as Christ says: Unless one is born
again, he cannot see the kingdom of God).[6]

Now, do all those strange saints of whom we hear—the
howling or chain-laden wandering dervishes, the Hindu
ascetics who torture their bodies, who stare into the
sun, hang themselves by their feet, or sit between five
fires, the Bengali *Aghori* who scrape out and consume
human corpses—do all of these belong in the same class
as Ramakrishna, Jakob Böhme, or Emanuel Swedenborg
(1688–1772)?

They are one and the same! Only at disparate stages. And
the processes through which the deaths of the 'accompa-
nying beings' occurs are unique for each individual, or are
striven for consciously in a variety of manners according to
the innumerable secret regulations of the diverse orders,
brotherhoods and sects.

Even if some act according to inner inspirations, to

the beckoning and orders they receive in dreams, to the Christian 'inner word', or through simply following a dark impulse, the result and the goal is always the same: *yoga*, the highest path of the true seeker. Because yoga is the end and not the beginning of the 'way', as so many believe today.

It may indeed happen that within the 'pilgrim' lesser miraculous powers suddenly manifest themselves when temporarily a small part of the aforementioned *formless force* is released. But these symptoms are not lasting. Instead, they are like the mirage in the desert, they are only the shadow that great events cast ahead.

They occur especially with all those who mistake the physical symptoms of the saints and almost-perfected yogis (as they are handed down in the vernacular or recorded as mudras, etc., in the writings of the Indian so-called *Hatha Yoga Pradipika*) for instructions, and endeavour to imitate them, confusing cause and effect. Instead of acquiring permanent powers, however, these unfortunates only form themselves into creatures standing between mediumism and true yogism—and then vanish.

*

Perhaps one day our science will succeed in precipitating the salts which lay solvent in these paths; then a formula will be quickly found offering the shortest route to (true) yoga. The realisation of a clear process, stripped of all tendrils, regarding how the aforementioned 'accompanying beings' (these parasites on the human psyche, of whose mere existence the present humanity has not the slightest idea) can be brought to death in the most expedient way—that would be the gain.

Notes to Introduction:

All English translations in footnoted entries by Frater Acher.

1 Henri Birven, p. 90.

2 Frans Smit, p. 154.

3 Gustav Meyrink, in an unpublished manuscript, in Frans Smit, pp. 200–201.

4 Gustav Meyrink, *Das Grüne Gesicht*, p. 168.

5 'To take by force...', an allusion to Matthew 11:12.

6 Frans Smit, pp. 225–226.

Primary sources:

Gustav Meyrink, *Der Golem*, 1915.

Das grüne Gesicht, 1917.

Der weiße Dominikaner. Aus dem Tagebuch eines Unsichtbaren, 1921.

Secondary sources:

Hartmut Binder, *Gustav Meyrink – Ein Leben im Bann der Magie*, 2009.

Henri Birven, *Gustav Meyrink als magisch-esoterischer Dichter*, 2020.

Camaysar; 'Von den Makifim – Entschlüssellung einer Textpassage aus dem "Grünen Gesicht" von G. Meyrink', in Frank Cebulla, Gundula Freytag (Eds.); *Der Golem*, 4. Jahrgang, Ausgabe No 11, 2003, pp. 18–26.

Alexandra David-Néel, *With Mystics and Magicians in Tibet*, 1936.

Theodor Harmsen, *Der magische Schriftsteller Gustav Meyrink, seine Freunde und sein Werk*, 2009.

Gershom Scholem, *Von der mystischen Gestalt der Gottheit*, 1995.

Frans Smit, *Gustav Meyrink – Auf der Suche nach dem Übersinnlichen*, 1988.

Papus, *Die Kabbala – Einführung in die jüdische Geheimlehre*, 1995.

Notes to *Fakir Paths*:

1 A reference to the 634th night from the classical collection of Middle Eastern folk-tales, *One Thousand and One Nights*.

2 For example, Ernst Mach.

3 Max Nordau, *Entartung*, 1892.

4 Geyrink does not cite his source.

5 Max Müller, *Ramakrishna: His Life and Sayings*, 1898.

6 An allusion to John 3:3.

qalatapi

whetstone

tuumoklawu

dream

aa'antsatawi

sacred song

ngámoki

medicine bundle

End Matter
Notes & Bibliography

New Work

Frater Acher
   The Straight Line is a Trap
Bede (Peter O'Leary, Trans.)
   Caedmon's Hymn
Sarah Berti
   Song of the Deermage
   Until the Omens Have Gone Dark
   At Midnight the Coywolves
   The Original Speech
   Translating Gods
Elizabeth-Jane Burnett
   Lupin Aphid
   Ghost Moth
Rebekah Clayton
   yew
Alton Melvar M. Dapanas
   Self-Portrait as Wak-wak
Kim Dorman
   Kerala Journal (Excerpts)
Rebecca Drake
   Awntyrs, women (Excerpt)
Michael Goodfellow
   Book of Days

Isidro Li
  Rio de Montaigne
  Excerpt from the Book of Waves and Fossils
  Nectere
  Solve et Coagula
Arvind Krishna Mehrotra
  Lockdown Garden (Excerpt)
Gustav Meyrink (Frater Acher, Trans.)
  Fakir Paths
Gaspar Orozco (Ilana Luna, Trans.)
  El Libro de los Espejismos / The Book of Mirages (Excerpts)
  Alminar / Minaret (Excerpt)
Triin Paja
  The Wrong Myth
  Daughters
  A Portrait of Old Animals
  Winter Farm
Paul Prudence
  Figured Stones (Excerpts)
Penelope Shuttle
  the half-guest
Richard Skinner
  Caedmon's Hymn
  A Patch of Birch
Jennifer Spector
  Song for the Nightshade
  A Little Way
Shash Trevett
  Waratah

Robin Walter
> *Pray not to behold*
> *Small reverie*
> *— Vein,*
> *— At the edge,*
> *— Across snow,*
> *Mercy of meadow*

Sarah Westcott
> *Bud*

Erin Wilson
> *Corm of Cyclamen*
> *Exigent, This: That*
> *In the Presence Of*

Archive Work

Natalie Curtis (Ed., Trans.)
> *The Indians' Book*, 1907

Don Domanski
> *Selected Poems, 1975-2021*, 2021

Frances Horovitz
> *Collected Poems: New Edition*, 2011

Kabir
> *One Hundred Poems of Kabir*, 1915

Donald A. Mackenzie
Myths of Babylonia and Assyria, 1915

Constance Naden
> *The Complete Poetical Works of Constance Naden*, 1894

William Tyler Olcott
> *Star Lore of All Ages*, 1911

Rabindranath Tagore
> *Stray Birds*, 1916

Word Lists

Words from *A Hopi-English Dictionary of the Third Mesa Dialect*, Bureau of Applied Research in Anthropology, University of Arizona, 1998.

Permissions

The poems of Frances Horovitz are reproduced with the kind permission of Bloodaxe Books.

Notes

Wherever possible, original spelling and punctuation have been preserved in the archive texts.

With Thanks

The editors would like to extend their thanks to the contributors, without whom *Reliquiae* would not be possible. They would also like to express heartfelt thanks to each *Friend* and *Patron* of Corbel Stone Press, whose continued support is most gratefully received.

Lightning Source UK Ltd.
Milton Keynes UK
UKHW010454100521
383373UK00001B/1